First World War
and Army of Occupation
War Diary
France, Belgium and Germany

51 DIVISION
153 Infantry Brigade,
Brigade Machine Gun Company
12 January 1916 - 28 February 1918

WO95/2882/3

The Naval & Military Press Ltd
www.nmarchive.com
Published in association with The National Archives

Published by

The Naval & Military Press Ltd

Unit 10 Ridgewood Industrial Park,

Uckfield, East Sussex,

TN22 5QE England

Tel: +44 (0) 1825 749494

www.naval-military-press.com

www.nmarchive.com

This diary has been reprinted in facsimile from the original. Any imperfections are inevitably reproduced and the quality may fall short of modern type and cartographic standards.

© **Crown Copyright**
Images reproduced by permission of The National Archives, London, England, 2015.

Contents

Document type	Place/Title	Date From	Date To
Heading	WO95/2882/3 153rd Brigade Machine Gun Company		
Heading	51st Division 153rd Machine Gun Coy Jan 1916-Feb 1918		
Heading	153 Bde M Gun Coy Jan & Feb Vol I		
Heading	153 Bde M G Coy Vol II		
Heading	153 Bde M G Coy Vol III		
War Diary	Fremont	12/01/1916	12/01/1916
War Diary	Vaux	20/01/1916	20/01/1916
War Diary	Fremont	25/01/1916	27/01/1916
War Diary	Corbie	06/02/1916	08/02/1916
War Diary	Bray	18/02/1916	28/02/1916
War Diary	Sailly-Le-Sec	29/02/1916	29/02/1916
War Diary	Cardonette	01/03/1916	01/03/1916
War Diary	Candas	06/03/1916	06/03/1916
War Diary	Doullens	09/03/1916	09/03/1916
War Diary	Oppy	10/03/1916	10/03/1916
War Diary	Maroeuil	11/03/1916	12/03/1916
War Diary	Bray	14/03/1916	28/04/1916
War Diary	N.Sector S Of Neuville St Vaast	05/05/1916	06/05/1916
War Diary	Bray	07/05/1916	19/05/1916
War Diary	N. Sector	20/05/1916	20/05/1916
War Diary	Aubigny	21/05/1916	21/05/1916
War Diary	Bray	27/05/1916	31/05/1916
War Diary	N.2.Sector	03/06/1916	22/06/1916
War Diary	M.2 Sector	22/06/1916	25/06/1916
War Diary	N2 Sector Zivy Redoubt	28/06/1916	28/06/1916
Heading	153rd Brigade 51st Division 153rd Brigade Machine Gun Company July 1916		
War Diary	Neuville St Vaast	02/07/1916	02/07/1916
War Diary	St. Vaast	13/07/1916	13/07/1916
War Diary	Bray	14/07/1916	14/07/1916
War Diary	Halloy	15/07/1916	15/07/1916
War Diary	Fienvillers	16/07/1916	20/07/1916
War Diary	Dernancourt	21/07/1916	21/07/1916
War Diary	Mametz Wood	22/07/1916	30/07/1916
War Diary	High Wood	30/07/1916	01/08/1916
War Diary	St Meaulte	02/08/1916	02/08/1916
Heading	153rd Brigade 51st Division 153rd Brigade Machine Gun Company August 1916		
War Diary	Meaulte	01/08/1916	06/08/1916
War Diary	Dernancourt	08/08/1916	08/08/1916
War Diary	Merlessart	09/08/1916	10/08/1916
War Diary	Wardrecques	11/08/1916	16/08/1916
War Diary	Armentieres	16/08/1916	31/08/1916
Heading	War Diary Of 153rd Coy Machine Gun Corps For Month Of September 1916 Volume 26		
War Diary	Armentieres	01/09/1916	09/09/1916
War Diary	Bailleul	10/09/1916	18/09/1916
War Diary	Armentieres	19/09/1916	25/09/1916
War Diary	Meteren	25/09/1916	30/09/1916

Heading	War Diary Of 153rd Company Machine Gun Corps From 1st October 1916 To 31st October 1916 (Volume9)		
War Diary	Beauval	01/10/1916	02/10/1916
War Diary	Vauchelles	02/10/1916	05/10/1916
War Diary	Louvencourt	06/10/1916	08/10/1916
War Diary	Bus-Les-Artois	08/10/1916	12/10/1916
War Diary	Colincamps	12/10/1916	17/10/1916
War Diary	Bus-Les-Artois	17/10/1916	18/10/1916
War Diary	Forceville	18/10/1916	08/11/1916
War Diary	Mailly-Maillet	11/11/1916	12/11/1916
War Diary	Beaumont Hamel	12/11/1916	15/11/1916
War Diary	Mailly-Maillet	15/11/1916	18/11/1916
War Diary	Raincheval	18/11/1916	18/11/1916
War Diary	Puichevillers	22/11/1916	23/11/1916
War Diary	Varennes	24/11/1916	30/11/1916
Heading	War Diary Of 153rd Company Machine Gun Corps From Dec 1'16 To Dec 31'16 Vol XI		
War Diary	Courcelette R.29. (Central)	01/12/1916	03/12/1916
War Diary	Ovillers Huts	03/12/1916	03/12/1916
War Diary	Bouzincourt	04/12/1916	04/12/1916
War Diary	Ovillers	10/12/1916	20/12/1916
War Diary	Courcelette R.29. (Central)	14/12/1916	20/12/1916
War Diary	Ovillers	20/12/1916	20/12/1916
War Diary	Bouzincourt	21/12/1916	21/12/1916
War Diary	Ovillers	28/12/1916	31/12/1916
Heading	War Diary Of 153rd Company Machine Gun Corps From Jany 1st 1917 To Jany 31st 1917 Volume 30		
War Diary	Ovillers	01/01/1917	02/01/1917
War Diary	Courcelette	03/01/1917	09/01/1917
War Diary	Ovillers	10/01/1917	10/01/1917
War Diary	Bouzincourt	10/01/1917	12/01/1917
War Diary	Puchevillers	14/01/1917	14/01/1917
War Diary	Bagneux	15/01/1917	15/01/1917
War Diary	Cramont	16/01/1917	16/01/1917
War Diary	Drucat	16/01/1917	16/01/1917
War Diary	Neuilly L'Hopital	19/01/1917	31/01/1917
Heading	War Diary Of 153rd Company Machine Gun Corps From Feb 1st 1917 To Feb 28th 1917 Volume 31		
War Diary	Neuilly L'Hopital	01/02/1917	04/02/1917
War Diary	Agenvillers	05/02/1917	05/02/1917
War Diary	Maison Ponthieu	06/02/1917	06/02/1917
War Diary	Haute Coute	07/02/1917	07/02/1917
War Diary	Hernicourt	08/02/1917	08/02/1917
War Diary	Dieval	09/02/1917	09/02/1917
War Diary	Caucourt	10/02/1917	10/02/1917
War Diary	Guestreville	11/02/1917	21/02/1917
War Diary	Bajus	21/02/1917	21/02/1917
War Diary	ACQ	21/02/1917	21/02/1917
War Diary	Frevin Capelle	21/02/1917	21/02/1917
War Diary	ACQ	21/02/1917	21/02/1917
War Diary	Bajus	22/02/1917	28/02/1917
Heading	War Diary Of 153rd Coy M G. Corps From 1st March To 31st March 1917 (Vol 15)		
War Diary	Bajus ACQ	01/03/1917	01/03/1917
War Diary	Ourton	02/03/1917	12/03/1917

War Diary	Bray	13/03/1917	15/03/1917
War Diary	In The Line	16/03/1917	16/03/1917
War Diary	Roclincourt Ecurie	16/03/1917	22/03/1917
War Diary	In The Line	23/03/1917	31/03/1917
Heading	War Diary Of 153rd Company Machine Gun Corps From 1st April 1917 To 30th April 1917 (Volume 33)		
War Diary	Roclincourt	01/04/1917	19/04/1917
War Diary	Fampoux	20/04/1917	24/04/1917
War Diary	Arras	25/04/1917	25/04/1917
War Diary	Marquay	26/04/1917	30/04/1917
Heading	War Diary Of 153rd Company Machine Gun Corps From 1st May 1917 To 31st May 1917 (Volume 34)		
War Diary	Marquay	01/05/1917	12/05/1917
War Diary	Arras	13/05/1917	13/05/1917
War Diary	Fampoux	14/05/1917	24/05/1917
War Diary	Arras	25/05/1917	29/05/1917
War Diary	Marquay	30/05/1917	31/05/1917
Heading	War Diary Of 153rd Company Machine Gun Corps From 1st June 1917 To 30th June 1917 (Volume 35)		
War Diary	Marquay	01/06/1917	03/06/1917
War Diary	Boyaval	04/06/1917	04/06/1917
War Diary	Erny St-Julien	05/06/1917	06/06/1917
War Diary	Wisernes	07/06/1917	07/06/1917
War Diary	Zudrove	08/06/1917	21/06/1917
War Diary	E Camp	22/06/1917	23/06/1917
War Diary	In Line	24/06/1917	30/06/1917
Heading	War Diary 153rd Coy Machine Gun Corps From 1st July 1917 To 31st July 1917 Volume 36		
War Diary	In The Line	01/07/1917	05/07/1917
War Diary	St Momelin	06/07/1917	22/07/1917
War Diary	Wind Mill Camp	23/07/1917	29/07/1917
War Diary	In The Line	29/07/1917	30/07/1917
Heading	War Diary Of 153rd Company Machine Gun Corps From 1st August 1917 To 31st August 1917 Volume 37		
War Diary	In The Line	01/08/1917	01/08/1917
War Diary	Siege Camp	02/08/1917	03/08/1917
War Diary	Z Camp	04/08/1917	04/08/1917
War Diary	St. Jan Ter Biezen	05/08/1917	29/08/1917
War Diary	Siege Camp	30/08/1917	31/08/1917
Heading	War Diary Of 153rd Company Machine Gun Corps From 1st Sept 1917 To 31st Sept 1917 (Volume 38)		
War Diary	Siege Camp	01/09/1917	06/09/1917
War Diary	Mentque	07/09/1917	10/09/1917
War Diary	Siege Camp	11/09/1917	14/09/1917
War Diary	In The Line	15/09/1917	21/09/1917
War Diary	'X' Camp	22/09/1917	29/09/1917
War Diary	Gomiecourt	30/09/1917	30/09/1917
Map	Map		
Heading	War Diary Of 153rd Company Machine Gun Corps From 1st Oct 1917 To 31st Oct 1917 (Volume 21)		
War Diary	Gomiecourt	01/10/1917	03/10/1917
War Diary	Coy H.Q In Line SE Of Arras (Cherisy Sector)	04/10/1917	15/10/1917
War Diary	Mercatel	16/10/1917	27/10/1917
War Diary	Wanquetin	28/10/1917	31/10/1917
Heading	153rd Brigade 51st Division 153rd Machine Gun Company November 1917		

Heading	War Diary Of 153rd Company Machine Gun Corps From 1st November To 30th November 1917 (Volume 22)		
War Diary	Wanquetin	01/11/1917	16/11/1917
War Diary	Beulencourt	17/11/1917	17/11/1917
War Diary	Metz	18/11/1917	18/11/1917
War Diary	Coy H.Q. Trescault	19/11/1917	21/11/1917
War Diary	Coy HQ In The Line	21/11/1917	30/11/1917
Miscellaneous	153rd Company Machine Gun Corps	27/11/1917	27/11/1917
Miscellaneous	War Diary Of 153rd Company, Machine Gun Corps From 1st December 1917 To 31st December 1917 (Volume 42)		
War Diary	Lechelle	01/12/1917	01/12/1917
War Diary	Flemicourt	02/12/1917	02/12/1917
War Diary	Coy HQ In The Line	03/12/1917	05/12/1917
War Diary	Favreuil	06/12/1917	06/12/1917
War Diary	Fremicourt	07/12/1917	10/12/1917
War Diary	Coy HQ In The Line	10/12/1917	16/12/1917
War Diary	Beugny	17/12/1917	21/12/1917
War Diary	Coy HQ Beugny	22/12/1917	22/12/1917
War Diary	Coy HQ In The Line	23/12/1917	31/12/1917
Heading	War Diary Of 153rd Company, Machine Gun Corps From 1st January 1918 To 31st January 1918 Volume 42		
War Diary	Coy HQ In Line (Pronville Sector)	01/01/1918	08/01/1918
War Diary	Coy HQ In The Line	09/01/1918	18/01/1918
War Diary	Beugny	19/01/1918	20/01/1918
War Diary	Courcelles Le Comte	21/01/1918	31/01/1918
Heading	War Diary Of 153rd Company Machine Gun Corps From 1st February 1918 To 28th February 1918 (Volume 43)		
War Diary	Courcelles-Le-Comte	01/02/1918	09/02/1918
War Diary	Coy HQ In The Line	10/02/1918	11/02/1918
War Diary	Coy HQ Morchies	12/02/1918	17/02/1918
War Diary	Company HQ Morchies	18/02/1918	28/02/1918

WO95/2882/3

53rd Brigade Machine Gun Company

51ST DIVISION

153RD MACHINE GUN COY.

JAN 1916-FEB 1918

51

153 Bde M Gun Coy

Jan & Feb

Vol I

153 Bde MG Coy

Vol II

51

153 Bde M.G. Coy

Vol. III

WAR DIARY or **INTELLIGENCE SUMMARY.**
(Erase heading not required.)

Army Form C. 2118.

153rd M.G. Company

Place	Date	Hour	Summary of Events and Information	Remarks and references to Appendices
TREMONT	12th Jan 1916	10.30 am	Formation of Company. M.G. Sections from Battalions rendezvoused at VAUX were met by Captain D.B. Calder, and marched to TREMONT, where Company went into billets. Officers who joined on formation. Captain Bro. Calder 16th Black Watch Bde Mg Officer. Commanding. Lieut. P. Le Brad 15th Gordon Highlanders. Lieut. A.D. Sbank 17th Gordon Highlanders. Lieut. R.L. Troup 15th Gordon Highlanders. Lieut. E.K. McDchail 17th Gordon Highlanders. Lieut. M. Wallace 17th Black Watch. Lieut. H.B. Dixon 16th Black Watch. Lieut. W.D. MacNaughton 16th Blackwatch. Lieut. D. Adamson 17th Blackwatch.	Nil.
VAUX	30th Jan	3.15 pm	Inspection of Transport by the Brigade Commander Gen'l Brigstre V.C.	
TREMONT	25th Jan	23	Inspection of Company billets by Brig Gen'l D. Campbell Bde Comdr	D36

Army Form C. 2118.

WAR DIARY
or
INTELLIGENCE SUMMARY.
(Erase heading not required.)

153rd Bde M.G. Company

Place	Date	Hour	Summary of Events and Information	Remarks and references to Appendices
TREMONT	27/1/16	10.15 am	Inspection of Company, transport etc by Major General G.M. Harper C.B. D.S.O.	D86
			During our stay at TREMONT the Coy was made a maxim Coy. 8 Vickers were handed to 152 Coy. and 8 maxims were received from 151 Coy.	
CORBIE	6/2/16	8.30 am	Company left TREMONT and marched to CORBIE.	D86
CORBIE	8/2/16	11.30 am	Company marched to SAILLY-LE-SEC. While here 8 Vickers received 8 maxims returned and Coy became a maxim & Vickers	D86
BRAY	18.2.16	12 noon	Proceeded to BRAY-SUR-SOMME.	
	19.2.16	5 pm	No. 4 Section under Lieut Sparks went into line at A. Ingoods but noted in trench at MARICOURT, relieving the 30th Division (16" MANCHESTER REGT 89th Brigade) 2 guns, there being no M.G. Coy in that Brigade.	
BRAY	20.2.16	5 pm	No. 2 Section under Lieut Smith (4 guns) took over MARICOURT defences from 89th Brigade. 2 guns were put into position. 2 were kept as mobile guns in a cellar.	
BRAY	28.2.16	12.30 am	Orders received to proceed out of the line. Two sections were relieved by Motor Machine Gun Battery and by 89th Bde Lewis guns.	
BRAY	28/2/16	1.15 pm	Company marched to SAILLY-LE-SEE arriving 6 pm. Roads in fearful condition	
SAILLY-LE-SEE	29/2/16	11 am	Company marched with 2 Brigade (Seaforth 15th, 17th Gordon High, Black Watch 9th) to CARDONETTE arriving 6.30 pm. Drivers were taken on the march, halting for one hour	

T2134. Wt. W708-776. 500000. 4/15. Sir J.C. & B.

SECRET

WAR DIARY

INTELLIGENCE SUMMARY

(Erase heading not required.)

Army Form C. 2118.

153 Coy. Machine Gun Corps

Place	Date	Hour	Summary of Events and Information	Remarks and references to Appendices
CARDONETTE	1/3/16		LIEUT. A.D. SPARK promoted Captain, and proceeded 1st October 1915.	
CANDAS	6/3/16	9.a.m	Marched to CANDAS. Captain Balder, Lieut Iorys went up with party to look over the French line.	
DOULLENS	9/3/16	11.a.m	Marched to DOULLENS.	
OPPY	10/3/16	11.a.m	Marched to OPPY.	
MAROEUIL	11/3/16	9.a.m	Marched to MAROEUIL. The weather during the past fortnight very inclement snow, frost, and rain alternating.	
MAROEUIL	12/3/16	6.p.m	16 guns went into the line taking over from the French. The sector is that between NEUVILLE-ST-VAAST and the LABYRINTH. An Army H.Q. is established in the trenches. Four Officers, and Orderly Room and Stores left behind at MAROEUIL, which the Transport Officer runs. Of the guns in the line, twelve are in support position, and four in Reserve. Great difficulty experienced lately owing to men evacuated. Company had to be made up by trained men from Battalions in Brigade. Transport drivers evacuated make it same difficulty.	

SECRET.

Army Form C. 2118.

WAR DIARY
or
INTELLIGENCE SUMMARY.
(Erase heading not required.)

153 bde Machine Gun Corps

Instructions regarding War Diaries and Intelligence Summaries are contained in F.S. Regs., Part II. and the Staff Manual respectively. Title pages will be prepared in manuscript.

Place	Date	Hour	Summary of Events and Information	Remarks and references to Appendices
MAROEUIL	12/3/16		Orders received authorising additional Officer in place of one to be made Second in Command. Captain O.L. Bird appointed Second in Command.	
BRAY	14/3/16		Orderly Room, Stores & Transport moved to BRAY. The new line M.G. positions very poor. Platforms all to be reconstructed to take our own Indirect Fire emplacements four in number, have been constructed.	
BRAY.	27/3/16		Draft of 7 men M.G. CORPS received from GRANTHAM. Consequent on orders received asking Territorial Coys to re-attest for Regular Army, for period of the War, papers have now been agreed by 1 W.Off. & men of this Company. There are still a few men, in Hospital, Convalescent Camp etc, who have yet to sign, but practically the whole Company has turned over to the Regular Army.	

David Hann .... CAPTAIN,
COMDG. 153RD BDE. M.G. COMPY.

Army Form C. 2118.

53 Coy Machine Gun Corps WAR DIARY or INTELLIGENCE SUMMARY.

Instructions regarding War Diaries and Intelligence Summaries are contained in F.S. Regs., Part II. and the Staff Manual respectively. Title pages will be prepared in manuscript.

(Erase heading not required.)

Place	Date	Hour	Summary of Events and Information	Remarks and references to Appendices
BRAY	4th April		Pte Brodie (No 1680) 1/7th Royal Highlanders attached, Killed by a stray bullet at MAISON BLANCHE	
"	6th April		3 Reinforcements M.G.C. joined the Company.	
"	9th "		"	
"	14th "		2 Lieut W D MacNaughton & 1 man to M.G. SCHOOL CAMIERS to course of instruction	
"	15th "		No. 10405 Pte A E Thomson, M.G.C. wounded, slight. High.	
"	16th "		Sergt. J McGregor Acting Sergt Major Sergt R Hannah A/ſmſgſ promoted Colour Sergt and appointed Coy Sergt Major & Coy Q Mſgſt to date.	
"	18th "		from 2.3.16.	
"	21st "		No. 9118 Pte Randle (Artificer) Joined Coy for duty	
"	25th "		Captain A.D. Spark & Sergt Sicks left for HAVRE to join a Class of instruction in Transport Duties.	
"	28th "		M.G.C. Orders received in which are detailed the Nos of 134 NCOs & men of this Coy on then transfer to the MACHINE GUN CORPS.	
			During the month, a great deal of hostile mining went on on our front. The Indirect M.G. positions were very useful on	

David Baeder [?] CAPTAIN
COMDG 153rd BDE. M.G. CORPS [?]

WAR DIARY
or
INTELLIGENCE SUMMARY.
(Erase heading not required.)

Army Form C. 2118.

153 Coy MACHINE GUN CORPS.

Place	Date	Hour	Summary of Events and Information	Remarks and references to Appendices

New schemes are being thought out on our BARRAGE LINES. Indeed the schemes were carried out extensively on enemy railway dumps, trenches, paths etc., and evidently considerable annoyance him, as his machine guns which had been practically silent since our taking over, have been quite busy lately. No. of rounds fired this month 146,650. Considerable trouble has been caused to us by breakage of Muzzle covers. A report was sent in to the Division on the matter. The Company has had a good record as regards sickness. Although all the neo's + men have been in the trenches since MARCH 13th there have only been 4 cases of sickness to end of April. The machines also which the Division did when coming up to this part of the line, although not many of this Company fell out from this Battalion.

There were a great number of men fell out from this Battalion.

A considerable amount of work has been done in the trenches as regards improvement of Gun emplacements, but they are still in a very unsatisfactory state.

David Slader

ORIGINAL
Vol 4

153 COY. MACHINE GUN CORPS WAR DIARY

INTELLIGENCE SUMMARY for MAY 1916.

Army Form C. 2118.

Place	Date	Hour	Summary of Events and Information	Remarks and references to Appendices
N. SECTOR. S of NEUVILLE ST VAAST.	5th May	3-30pm	No. 20210 Pte J. Milne Killed in action. A trench mortar bomb landed on our emplacement, going right through. No. 20201 Pte H. Church was at the same time slightly wounded.	
"	6th May		Some damage to equipment caused by shell fire, a shell bursting just behind our emplacement.	
BRAY	7th May		Reinforcement of 1 Pte arrived from CAMIERES.	
"	11th May		No. 20201 Pte H. Church wounded on 5th inst., rejoined for duty.	
"	19th "		Lieut G.J. Smith arrived from CAMIERS to complete establishment.	
N. SECTOR	20th		CASUALTIES. No. 20142 L/Cpl D. Hunter No. 20152 Pte H. Birmingham, Killed in action, both buried in cemetery at MAROEUIL. No. 20224 Pte W. Grundy wounded. No. 20137 Pte L. Young wounded. Trench mortar bomb shelter. All by shell fire.	
AUBIGNY	21st		No. 20224 Pte W. Grundy died of wounds.	
BRAY	27th		M.G.C. orders received notify Gazette of Captain P.C. Bird of the Company to be Second-in Command. dated 24th Feby. 1916.	
BRAY	31st		During the month the chief operations carried out have been	

David Ballell CAPTAIN,
COMDG. 153RD BDE. M.G. COMPY.

ORIGINAL

Army Form C. 2118.

153 COY. M.G. CORPS. (cont'd) WAR DIARY.
INTELLIGENCE SUMMARY. 1st MAY. 1916.

(Erase heading not required.)

Instructions regarding War Diaries and Intelligence Summaries are contained in F. S. Regs., Part II. and the Staff Manual respectively. Title pages will be prepared in manuscript.

Place	Date	Hour	Summary of Events and Information	Remarks and references to Appendices
BRAY.	31st May		Indirect fire schemes on enemy's Reserve trenches, roads, paths, dumps etc. 42,000 rds have been expended.	
			On this date the Company has completed its 80th Consecutive day in the trenches, as owing to all our gun-teams in the men have not been relieved. Part of a new Sector (M.2) was taken into our Brigade Area and we now have gun distributed as follows	
			M.2. (right of Brigade.) 2 guns in SUPPORT LINE.	
			N.1. 5 guns in firing line 2 in SUPPORT. 1 in RESERVE 2 in OVERHEAD position.	
			N.2. 2 guns in SUPPORT LINE.	
			BRIGADE RESERVE. 2 guns.	
			TRENCH COY HD. QRS. SAPPEUR SHELTERS, N.1.	
			COY. REAR HD QRS. ORDERLY ROOM STORES TRANSPORT at BRAY.	
			All Trench Nos are in reference to TRENCH MAP. ROCLINCOURT. 51.B 1/10,000	

David Baker Capt
COMDG. 153rd BDE. M.G. COY.

153rd Company M.G. Corps.

Army Form C. 2118.

WAR DIARY
or
INTELLIGENCE SUMMARY.

(Erase heading not required.)

to June 1916.

Pt 5

Place	Date	Hour	Summary of Events and Information	Remarks and references to Appendices
N.2. Sector	3rd	9 P.M.	A raid was carried out by the 1/7 Black Watch on the German trenches opposite this Sector. The guns of this Company co-operated very successfully.	
	8th		Notification received that the Company under my command will be armed with Short Rifles.	
	22nd		Saddlers and Transport Driver (from GRANTHAM) taken on the Company Strength.	
M.2 Sector	22nd	7.30PM	The following men were wounded by a Trench mortar bomb, which exploded immediately on the top of "H" Gun Emplacement. No 20222 Pte W. Todd. No 10251 Pte J. Farrell. No 10403 Pte W. Spinks. No 20162 Pte W. Roberton	
	25th		Company Armed with Vickers Guns having previously been ½ maxim ½ Vickers completion.	
N.2 Sector	28th	2 P.M.	The following men were wounded by a .77 H.E. Shell which passed through the loophole of the Emplacement. No 2020 Pte A. Reid (1/5 Gordon Highlanders) attached to the Company under my command for duty. No 492 Pte J Wilson (1/7 Gordon Highlanders) ditto ditto.	

David Rowde.
CAPTAIN,
COMDG. 153RD BDE. M.G. COMPY.

153rd Brigade.

51st Division.

153rd BRIGADE MACHINE GUN COMPANY

JULY 1 9 1 6

WAR DIARY
~~INTELLIGENCE~~ SUMMARY.
(Erase heading not required.)

Army Form C. 2118.

Vol 6

153 COY. MACHINE GUN CORPS

Place	Date	Hour	Summary of Events and Information	Remarks and references to Appendices
	1916			
NEUVILLE ST VAAST.	2nd July		179 COY. M.G. CORPS attached for Instruction.	
	13th "		Handed over to 179 COY, and my boy went back to BRAY. The N.C.O.s and men of 153 COY had been in the trenches continuously, without relief for 134 days.	
BRAY.	14th July		Marched to ROCOURT ST LAURENT. 14 miles to billets. Arrived about 2-30 p.m. At 5 p.m. got orders to be ready to move off in motor lorries by 7-30 p.m. Transport to go by road. Owing to our lorries being taken by one of the battalions we did not get away until about 11-30 p.m.	
HALLOY	15th July		Arrived about 4 a.m. Stayed here all day.	
FIENVILLERS	16th July		Marched from HALLOY at 9.30 a.m. and marched to FIENVILLERS passing through DOULLENS. Stayed in FIENVILLERS till 20th.	
FIENVILLERS	19th July		Orders came from BRIGADE to send on transport by road to FLESSELLES.	
FIENVILLERS	20th July		Coy entrained at CANDAS at 4 p.m. and detrained about 9 p.m. at MERICOURT thence marching to DERNANCOURT.	
DERNANCOURT	21st July		Brigade went into General Reserve at MAMETZ wood. 153 Coy. served the 99th Coy 33rd Division.	

David B Leeds
COMDG 153 B COY...

Army Form C. 2118.

WAR DIARY

INTELLIGENCE SUMMARY.

(Erase heading not required.)

153 COY. MACHINE GUN CORPS.

Instructions regarding War Diaries and Intelligence Summaries are contained in F. S. Regs., Part II. and the Staff Manual respectively. Title pages will be prepared in manuscript.

Place	Date	Hour	Summary of Events and Information	Remarks and references to Appendices
	1916			
MAMETZ WOOD	22nd Jul to 25th Jul		Lay in Reserve. Shelled daily, and had two nights of gas shells. Box respirators were found to be ample protection and had no casualties from these shells. During these 4 days the following casualties occurred to my Coy. KILLED - nil. WOUNDED 2. Other ranks	
	26th July		Brigade took over HIGH WOOD Sector of front line. Coy. had 5 guns in front line, 7 guns in support line between MILL near BAZENTIN LE PETIT through BAZENTIN LE GRAND and along French gunpits E towards LONGUEVAL. 4 guns were in Brigade Reserve at MAMETZ wood. Lieuts Drouts & Adamson 4 guns nos. 1 of no 4 in front line. Captain Spark & Lieut McPhail. 3 guns no 4 + of no 1. in support line. Casualties. 3 KILLED. Other ranks. 1 O.R. Wounded.	
	27th July		" 1 KILLED.	
	28th "		" 2 WOUNDED	
	29th "		" at HIGH WOOD	
	30th July 6.10 pm		Brigade attacked GERMAN LINE. Attack failed. I had relieved the 2nd line guns in morning. The distribution before attack was. Captain Spark, Lieuts Adamson & Dixon went into 2nd line with 3 guns	

Sunderland
CAPTAIN
COMDG. 153RD COY.

Army Form C. 2118.

WAR DIARY
INTELLIGENCE SUMMARY.
(Erase heading not required.)

153. COY. MACHINE GUN CORPS

Place	Date	Hour	Summary of Events and Information	Remarks and references to Appendices
HIGH WOOD	1916 30th July		of No.4 Section and 2 guns of No.1. In Support line 2 guns of No.1. 4 of No.3 and 1 of No.4 under Lieuts Troup McPhail Adamson. 4 guns of No.2 and Coy HD QRS in BAZENTIN LE GRAND. The orders were that 3 guns would advance after the infantry had attained their objective and during the consolidation of the line. The other 2 guns in 3rd line were on W side of HIGH WOOD. They were to fire over front to be attacked by 19th Div. 1 gun in support were to fire indirect fire on enemy communications. The infantry over got forward but eventually retired back of the distance and had to stay there. The three guns all got parties forward, and the 2 old line. The three guns all got parties forward, and the arrangements made beforehand were well carried out. Two extra guns were sent up from Support during the night as reinforcements.	
MEAULTE	1st August		Relieved by 152 Coy. our Brigade then going back to camp near MEAULTE. CASUALTIES on 30th KILLED 4. Other ranks WOUNDED 9	

David Baxter CAPTAIN
COMDG. 153RD BDE. M.G. COMPY

Army Form C. 2118.

WAR DIARY

INTELLIGENCE SUMMARY.
(Erase heading not required.)

153 COY. MACHINE GUN CORPS

Place	Date	Hour	Summary of Events and Information	Remarks and references to Appendices
At MEAULTE	1916 Aug 9th		During the eleven days in the line, the gun casualties were: 2 guns out of action. One hit by shrapnel and bullet in barrel casing. One check lever plate broken. Two tripods knocked out. It was found that by taking over belt boxes and handing over the like number was the only practical way to relieve, as there are not enough men to carry in all the belt boxes. RECOMMENDATIONS. Captain A.D. Spark. D.S.O. Lieut. Adamson Military Cross. Pte. Newton. L.C. Laird Military Medal.	

David Spark
COMDG. 153 ... CAPTAIN

153rd Brigade.
51st Division.

153rd BRIGADE MACHINE GUN COMPANY

AUGUST 1 9 1 6 ::::

ORIGINAL

Army Form C. 2118.

CONFIDENTIAL
No 81 (A)
HIGHLAND
DIVISION

WAR DIARY
or
~~INTELLIGENCE SUMMARY.~~
(Erase heading not required.)

Instructions regarding War Diaries and Intelligence Summaries are contained in F. S. Regs., Part II. and the Staff Manual respectively. Title pages will be prepared in manuscript.

Place	Date	Hour	Summary of Events and Information	Remarks and references to Appendices
	AUGUST			
MEAULTE	1st	10 PM	Relieved by the 152nd Company, Machine Gun Corps and went into Camp near MEAULTE	PLB
	2nd		Reinforcement of one Sergeant and six men	PLB
	6th		Reinforcement of two Lance Corporals and nineteen men marched back to Camp near DERNANCOURT on ALBERT - AMIENS ROAD.	PLB
DERNANCOURT	8th	4.30 PM	Transport left by road for MERLESSART, staying for the night at POULAINVILLE on route to MERLESSART.	PLB
MERLESSART.	9th		The Company entrained at MERICOURT about 3 P.M. and marched to MERLESSART. The Officers were in billets, other ranks bivouaced out, the weather was rather inclement.	PLB PLB
	10th		The Company marched to LONGPRÉ and entrained at 12 midnight, going via BOULOGNE, CALAIS, ST OMER, HASEBROUCK -	PLB
WARDRECQUES	11th		The Company detrained at THIENNES and marched to WARDRECQUES.	PLB
	12th		2nd Lieut NUTT and 6 O.R. joined	PLB
	13th		2nd Lieut. W. D. MACNAUGHTON evacuated sick. Lieut. R. J. TROUP left for CAMIERS for duty at Machine Gun School.	PLB

T.2134. Wt. W708—776. 500000. 4/15. Sir J. C. & S.

Army Form C. 2118.

WAR DIARY
or
INTELLIGENCE SUMMARY
(Erase heading not required.)

Instructions regarding War Diaries and Intelligence Summaries are contained in F. S. Regs., Part II. and the Staff Manual respectively. Title pages will be prepared in manuscript.

Place	Date	Hour	Summary of Events and Information	Remarks and references to Appendices
	AUGUST			
WARDRECQUES	15th		A reinforcement of 2 Lance Corporals and 18 men joined.	P.B.
	16th	5 a.m.	Transport moved from WARDRECQUES to ARMENTIÈRES by road, arriving about 11 p.m. They billeted near LES 3 TAILLEULS.	P.B.
		9 a.m.	The Commanding Officer left with Captain A.D. Spark by motor lorry to inspect the line.	P.B.
		1.40 p.m.	The dismounted personnel paraded under Captain P.C. Bird, entrained at EBBLINGHAM, the train starting at 4 p.m. Detrained at STEENWERCK, and marched to ARMENTIÈRES, arriving about 8 p.m.	P.B.
ARMENTIÈRES	16/17th midnight		Captain A.D. Spark took guns &c up to Headquarters where they were dumped	P.B. P.B.
	17th	5 a.m.	The Company marched up to the line and took over from 2nd Anzac Machine Gun Company (Captain Parks O.C. this Company)	P.B.
	18th		500 rounds fired (Indirect) on enemy lines.	P.B.
	19th		2,600 rounds fired (Indirect) at Cross Roads at LE FELOT, LES HALLOTS FARM (direct), and FRELINGHIEM. Work is carried out improving gun platforms and strengthening positions, and constructing shelters. 201.39 Sergeant Rogers wounded.	P.B. P.B.
	20th			

Army Form C. 2118.

WAR DIARY
or
INTELLIGENCE SUMMARY.
(Erase heading not required.)

153 COMPANY, Machine Gun Corps

Place	Date	Hour	Summary of Events and Information	Remarks and references to Appendices
AUGUST				
ARMENTIERES	21st		1000 rounds (Indirect) fired on FRELINGHIEN at 500 at FME DU CHASSEE	PMcB
	22nd		20180 Lance-Corporal Forsyth wounded, self-inflicted.	PMcB
	24th		Six alternative machine gun emplacements completed.	BB
	28th		Captain A.D. Spark left to command 4th Machine Gun Company. 2nd Lieut. W.D. Macnaughton returned from hospital.	PMcB
	28th		42118 Pte Mackenzie J. wounded. 34185 Pte Fitzsimmons J. (artificer) gassed	PMcB
	31st	1.30am	Machine guns successfully cooperated in gas attack, some enemy fire to drown sound of escaping gas. 20119 Pte Comrie D. wounded.	PMcB
	22nd/31st		39,280 rounds have been fired during this period at working parties &c. and indirectly at the enemy support and reserve lines, roads and crossroads. Places such as FME DU CHASTEL, LA HOULETTE, FME DES OURSINS, HOBBS FME, LE FELOT. Work was carried in trenches, saps, lilos, latrines and mutual aid, making shelter, strengthening emplacements, constructing alternative emplacements and firing shields in emplacements.	PMcB

P McB.......... CAPTAIN,
COMDG. 153RD M.G. COMPY.

Vol 8

War Diary
of
153rd Coy. Machine Gun Corps
for month of September 1916.

Volume 26.

Original

Army Form C. 2118.

WAR DIARY
or
INTELLIGENCE SUMMARY.
(Erase heading not required.)

153 M.G. Company

Place	Date	Hour	Summary of Events and Information	Remarks and references to Appendices
ARMENTIERES	SEPTEMBER 1st		Company in the line. A Gas Attack was made on enemy lines. M.G. fire was employed to deaden sound of escaping gas. Enemy replied with very weak Artillery & M.G. fire. Overhead fire carried out nightly on Cross Roads, Railways etc. behind enemy lines. Rounds fired in Indirect Fire from 1st – 9th – 26,300	
	3rd		Lieut. WALLACE struck off strength of Coy – to ENGLAND –	
	9th		Company relieved by 154 Coy. Capt. D.B. Calder – to be seconded from being Bde. M.G. Officer to M.G. Corps	
BAILLEUL	10th		Company marched to BAILLEUL. Camped out under Canvas.	
	14th		Lieut. G.R. McPhail appointed 2nd in Command 91st M.G. Coy	
	17th		Capt. D.B. Calder to be temp Major while in command Ja M.G. Coy Inspection of Coy. by S.O.C. 51st Division	
	18th	3.30 p.m	Marched to ARMENTIERES. The Commanding Officer and another Adamson left by M6th Bus at 8 AM to go round new line prior to taking over from 152 Coy.	

Army Form C. 2118.

WAR DIARY
or
INTELLIGENCE SUMMARY.
(Erase heading not required.)

153 M.G. Coy

Place	Date	Hour	Summary of Events and Information	Remarks and references to Appendices
ARMENTIERES	SEPT. 19th	11 AM	Relief of 152 Coy completed. No.1 Section, Q.M. store etc. in ARMENTIERES	
	20th		2nd Lieut. MacNaughton returned from leave.	
	22nd		No. 8194 Pte. Tyler S. Accidentally wounded. Indirect Fire was carried out nightly on enemy dumps, roads used for Relieving Ration parties etc. Ammunition expended 27,000 rds. Enemy's attitude opposite our Section was extremely quiet. Very little Artillery fire. However his Minnenwerfer were frequently employed against our front line.	
	24th		Company relieved by 103 M.G. Coy. System of Relief in the Section was as follows:— On Brigade previous to Relief, Relieving Company took guns & equipment up to trenches in limbers. When they were dumped. Next day Company would march up to the Dump and collect the guns & equipment. The same system was carried out by the Company being relieved. Capt. P. C. Bott left to command 64 M.G. Coy	
	25th		Company marched to METEREN.	

Army Form C. 2118.

WAR DIARY
or
INTELLIGENCE SUMMARY.
(Erase heading not required.)

Instructions regarding War Diaries and Intelligence Summaries are contained in F. S. Regs., Part II. and the Staff Manual respectively. Title pages will be prepared in manuscript.

Place	Date	Hour	Summary of Events and Information	Remarks and references to Appendices
METEREN	SEPT. 25th to 30th		Company Training in following :- Tactical handling of M. Guns in attack and defence. Visual training. Route Marching etc.	
	10th		The following G. Officers joined the Company during the month :- Lieut. J. R. RUSSEL from G. RANTHAM. 2nd Lieut. W. E. S. NAPIER joined as 2nd in Command from 74 M.G. Coy.	
	30th	3.28 p.m	The Company entrained at BAILLEUL. Arrived DOULLENS at 9 p.m. Marched to BERNAVILLE where they arrived 11.30 p.m	

David Blackden MAJOR
COMDG. 153RD M.G. COMPY.

CONFIDENTIAL.

WAR DIARY.

OF

153rd. COMPANY MACHINE GUN CORPS.

FROM 1st OCTOBER, 1916. to 31st OCTOBER, 1916.

(VOLUME 27)

Army Form C. 2118.

WAR DIARY
or
INTELLIGENCE SUMMARY.
(Erase heading not required.)

1/5-3 Coy, M.G. Corps

Instructions regarding War Diaries and Intelligence Summaries are contained in F.S. Regs, Part II. and the Staff Manual respectively. Title pages will be prepared in manuscript.

Place	Date	Hour	Summary of Events and Information	Remarks and references to Appendices
	OCTOBER			
BEAUVAL	1	—	Company Training & Cleaning up	
	2	10.30 AM	Marched to VAUCHELLES-les-AUTHIE, via BEAUQUESNE, MARIEUX	
VAUCHELLES		3.15 PM	Arrived	
	5	10 AM	Marched to LOUVENCOURT	
LOUVENCOURT		10.40 AM	Arrived	
	5-8		Attack Practice was carried out over ground laid off to represent a certain portion of the German front line system near SERRE	
	8	12.45 PM	Marched to BUS-les-ARTOIS	
BUS-les-ARTOIS		2.80 PM	Arrived	
	9		Lieut. N.F. DIXON appointed 2nd in Command 64 M.G. Coy	
	9-11		Attack practice	
	9		2nd Lt. G. EADIE, 8/11th Royal Scots, joined the Coy. from the Base.	
	12"	2.30 PM	Marched to COHINCAMPS	
COHINCAMPS	12"	5 PM	Coy H.Q in a Barn. Three Section in the lin, relieved one Section of 154 Coy	
	12-16		Section in the line, relieved one Section of 15th Coy. 11,000 Rounds were expended in Indirect Fire. The following	

T/134. Wt. W708-776. 500000. 4/15. Sir J. C. & S.

WAR DIARY
or
INTELLIGENCE SUMMARY.
(Erase heading not required.)

153 M.G. Coy

Army Form C. 2118.

Place	Date	Hour	Summary of Events and Information	Remarks and references to Appendices
	OCTOBER			Map Ref. HEBUTERNE 57 D. N.E 3 & 4 1/10,000
COLINCAMPS	12-16		Points were particularly fired at :- BOX WOOD, STAR WOOD, C.T.s behind THE POINT, LA LOUVIERE Farm.	
"	17		Relieved by 9th M.G Coy. Marched to BUS	
BUS-to-ARTGS	18	12.30pm	Arrived.	
		9AM	Marched to FORCEVILLE	
FORCEVILLE	"	1pm	Arrived.	
"	20	12.30pm	H.Qr. No. 2 Section relieved No. 1 Section of 152 Coy. in front of BEAUMONT HAMEL. Rear of Coy in bivouacs in wood R.17.c.3.6	
	27		No. 4 Section relieved No. 2 Section in the line.	
	29		No. 1 Section went into the line.	
	20-31		During this period, enemy wire have been cut in a great many places, M.G fire was directed on the wire in order to prevent its being repaired. Some Indirect fire was also carried out, chiefly on BEAUMONT HAMEL and the roads leading from it, WAGGON & STATION Roads. Rounds expended 25,000	

DavidBlaeder MAJOR
COMDG. 153rd COY. M.G. CORPS.

51.

WC/10 Army Form C. 2118.

WAR DIARY
or
INTELLIGENCE SUMMARY.
(Erase heading not required.)

153 Company, Machine Gun Corps

Place	Date	Hour	Summary of Events and Information	Remarks and references to Appendices
	November			
FORCEVILLE	1-5		Company headquarters remain at Forceville. Guns in line fire 32,000 rounds on enemy trenches and communication lines.	
	5		March to RAINCHEVAL and ACHEUX and LEALVILLERS	
	7		No 3 Section comes out of line relieved by section of 154 M.G.C. 4 O.R. join	
	8		19 O.R. join 153 M.G.C. from 4 battalions of the brigade. 19000 rounds fired in line	
MAILLY-MAILLET	9-10	noon	Company marches to MAILLY-MAILLET	
BEAUMONT HAMEL	9-12		35,000 rounds fired (indirect) on enemy targets	
	12	2 a.m.	Company goes into line and Nos 1,3, 2 & 4 sections make preparations for overhead fire. No 2 section with 4 guns moved from overhead position into the line	
		2 p.m.	Major Calder (C.O.) with 2nd Lt. D.G. Nutt, opened Ley Hd gun in line	
	13	5.45 a.m.	Artillery and M.G. barrage from 12 guns then covering advancing infantry. 2nd Lt. D.F. ADAMSON and 2nd Lt. G.S. SMITH advance on right flank of each attacking battalion.	
		8 a.m.	2nd Lt. ADAMSON wounded and one of this guns out of action. Information received that 2nd Lt. SMITH's guns both out of action, one lost, the other returned. 3 L. Sgts. killed	
		8.30 a.m.	Lieut. RUSSELL goes forward to firing line	
		9.20 a.m.	2nd Lt. MACNAUGHTON goes up with four guns of No 3 section, two remain with brigade headquarters and two are sent to 1/6 BLACK WATCH.	

Army Form C. 2118.

WAR DIARY (Cont.)
or
INTELLIGENCE SUMMARY

(Erase heading not required.) 153 Company, Machine Gun Corps

Instructions regarding War Diaries and Intelligence Summaries are contained in F. S. Regs., Part II. and the Staff Manual respectively. Title pages will be prepared in manuscript.

Place	Date	Hour	Summary of Events and Information	Remarks and references to Appendices
	November			
BEAUMONT HAMEL	13	noon	Information received that Lieut. RUSSELL is wounded and his guns are still in old front line with part of 1/6 BLACK WATCH.	
			Situation at this time was that 4 guns of no1 section and 2 of no 3 were in front of Y ravine and were held up with infantry. One gun sends no information.	
		5 p.m.	A corporal and two men return with gun covered with mud. They were held up in a shell hole and detained at bath as gun was covered with mud.	
		8 p.m.	Operation orders received. 2nd Lt. NUTT and 2nd Lt. MACNAUGHTON with four guns go forward in the darkness under an intermittent hostile shell fire and take up their positions in the old German third line.	
	14	1.30 a.m.	News received at headquarters that 4 guns have been put into position in third line.	
	14-15		No change in situation. Search parties recovered the two guns which had been lost.	
			Casualties; Killed 2nd Lt. G.S. SMITH.	
			Wounded: 2nd Lt. D.F. ADAMSON.) Lieut. J.R. RUSSELL.	
			No. of rounds fired in barrage fire - 46,000.	
MAILLY-MAILLET	15		152 Machine Gun Company relieves this company, which proceeds to MAILLY-MAILLET	
	15-18		Reorganization and re-equipment of company.	

Army Form C. 2118.

WAR DIARY
or
INTELLIGENCE SUMMARY.
(Erase heading not required.)

153 Company Machine Gun Corps

Place	Date	Hour	Summary of Events and Information	Remarks and references to Appendices
	November			
RAINCHEVAL	18		Company marches to RAINCHEVAL via ACHEUX and LEAVILLERS. 20 O.R. join from Base.	
			2nd Lt. H.H. BRAY, 2nd Lt. G.A. AINSWORTH, 2nd Lt. W.M. HASTWELL join.	
PUICHEVILLERS	22		Company marches to PUICHEVILLERS.	
	23		2nd Lt. E.V. RIDGE joins.	
VARENNES	24		Company marches to VARENNES	
	26		No 3 section goes into line at COURCELETTE; remainder of company to huts near AVELUY.	
	27		No 1 and 4 sections go into line	
	28		No 2 section goes into line to relieve no 3 section	
	29		Two Sections of the 157th Coy. come to this Company for furtyre	
	30		barrage fire. 20,000 rounds fired.	

Montagu[?]
COMDG. 153rd COY. M.G. CORPS.

Vol XI

CONFIDENTIAL

WAR · DIARY ·

of

153rd Company, MACHINE GUN CORPS.

FROM DEC.1/16 to DEC 31/16

VOL 29

Army Form C. 2118.

No 711(A) HIGHLAND DIVISION
153 Machine Gun Company.

WAR DIARY
or
INTELLIGENCE SUMMARY.
(Erase heading not required.)

Instructions regarding War Diaries and Intelligence Summaries are contained in F. S. Regs., Part II. and the Staff Manual respectively. Title pages will be prepared in manuscript.

Place	Date	Hour	Summary of Events and Information	Remarks and references to Appendices
	December.			
COURCELETTE R 29 (Central)	1-3. 1-3.		Nos. 1, 2 - 4 Sections in the line with 2 Sections attacked from 154 Machine Gun Company. OPERATIONS:- 48,000 rounds were fired (machine) by right and left groups of "Barrage Guns" on WEST and EAST MIRAUMONT and the outskirts of PYS. During this time in the line, the Trenches were in an indescribable condition & were unable to be used on any occasion. Casualties 2 ORs Wounded	
OVILLERS HUTS	3.		Company relieved by 154 Machine Gun Company.	
BOUZINCOURT	4.		Company marched to Billets in BOUZINCOURT. (Reserve Area)	
OVILLERS	10.		Company moved to WORSLEY HUTS.	
	14.		Company relieved No. 152 Machine Gun Company - Nos 3 - 4 Sections go into the line	
	17.		Nos. 3 - 4 Sections relieved by Nos 1. 2. Sections.	
	14-20.		Company in the line Gun Positions: Right front - 4 Barrage Guns - 3 Forward Positions. Left front - 4 Barrage Guns - 2 KENORA TRENCH. 2 Front Line. 2 Guns in Reserve.	

WAR DIARY
or
INTELLIGENCE SUMMARY.
(Erase heading not required.)

Army Form C. 2118.

153 Machine Gun Company.

Place	Date	Hour	Summary of Events and Information	Remarks and references to Appendices
December				
COURCELETTE	14-20		During this tour in the trenches 30,000 rounds were fired	1/10000 LE SARS
R.29 (Centre)			EAST - WEST MIRAUMONT ROADS - outskirts of PYS.	
			Squares R 10-11-12 - Roads M.8.c' M.7.d'.	
			For the first few days the trenches were in a very bad condition, but the heavy frost during the latter few days improved conditions considerably.	
			Casualties - 1 Sergt - 10 R wounded.	
OVILLERS	20		The company was relieved by the 154 Machine Gun Company.	
BOUZINCOURT	21.		The company moved into billets at BOUZINCOURT.	
	22		Q.M. Wole joins.	
			On the 26th November Major D.B. Caldwell proceeded to GHQ M.G. school at Camiers and has since been mutilated to ENGLAND.	
OVILLERS	28.		The company moved into support area at WORSLEY HUTS.	
	28-31		Working Parties were sent to 152 Machine Gun Company to assist with work in the line	

W Napier MAJOR
COMDG. 153RD COY M.G. CORPS.

CONFIDENTIAL
No. 21(A)
HIGHLAND DIVISION

War Diary

of

153rd. Company, Machine Gun Corps.

From Jany 1st: 1917 to Jany: 31st: 1917.

Volume 30

Army Form C. 2118.

WAR DIARY
or
INTELLIGENCE SUMMARY.
(Erase heading not required.)

EXHIBIT
No 21(A)
HIGHLAND DIVISION
153 Machine Gun Coy

Instructions regarding War Diaries and Intelligence Summaries are contained in F.S. Regs., Part II. and the Staff Manual respectively. Title pages will be prepared in manuscript.

Place	Date	Hour	Summary of Events and Information	Remarks and references to Appendices
	JANUARY			
OVILLERS	1-2		Supplied working parties & 1 officer + 20 men for 152 M.G. Coy who were in the line.	Ref MAP LESARS 1/10,000
COURCELETTE	3-9	9ª	Relieved 152 M.G. Coy in the line. 7 guns in support Line. 6 " " " Overhead Fire. 2 " " Reserve 2 Coy 16.9. #1 " " " Guns were manned with 1 N.C.O. + 3 men which allowed an interval relief at end of 3 days. The remaining men & guns were kept in shelters at Res Coy 16.9. Operations:- 3,000 Rounds were fired nightly on enemy's communication & dumps. Targets were mostly chosen from Aeroplane Photos & Intelligence Reports. W.O.R.K. Work on def: dugouts & cover was continued, 6 R.E.'s being but by Pioneer Battalion for supervision of work on dugouts. Enemy's Machine Guns were notably inactive, a little attention being paid however to the E. of MIRAUMONT Rd. and Dy KEVAH ET. No overhead fire was carried on by day.	

2353 Wt. W2544/1454 700,000 5/15 D.D.&L. A.D.S.S./Forms/C. 2118.

Army Form C. 2118.

WAR DIARY
or
INTELLIGENCE SUMMARY.
(Erase heading not required.)

15-3 M.G. Coy.

Instructions regarding War Diaries and Intelligence Summaries are contained in F. S. Regs., Part II. and the Staff Manual respectively. Title pages will be prepared in manuscript.

Place	Date	Hour	Summary of Events and Information	Remarks and references to Appendices
	JANUARY			
COURCELETTE	9	9ᵃ	Relieved by 154 M.G. Coy. To nr. OVILLERS	
OVILLERS	10	10ᴬᴹ	March to BOUZINCOURT	
BOUZINCOURT	10	12ᴬᴹ	Arrived	
	12		Left BOUZINCOURT	
PUCHEVILLERS			Arrived	
	14		Left PUCHEVILLERS	
BAGNEUX			Arrived	
	15		Left BAGNEUX	
CRAMONT			Arrived	
	16		Left CRAMONT	
DRUCAT			Arrived	
NEUILLY L'HOPITAL	19		Arrived from DRUCAT	
	19-31		Reorganisation & training	

W.N. Apwh
A. Comdg. 153ʳᵈ Coy. M.G. Corps.

Vol 13

CONFIDENTIAL

WAR DIARY.
of
153rd COMPANY, MACHINE GUN CORPS.

FROM FEB. 1st 1917 to FEB. 28th 1917.

VOLUME 31

Army Form C. 2118.

WAR DIARY
or
INTELLIGENCE SUMMARY.
(Erase heading not required.)

153 Machine Gun Coy.

Place	Date	Hour	Summary of Events and Information	Remarks and references to Appendices
FEBRUARY				
NEUILLY L'HOPITAL	1-4		1st Brigade field day. Attack practice on brigade training area. All guns employed. 2nd. The same practice repeated before Corps General and Divisional General. 3rd. Company paraded at DRUCAT where General Officer Commanding 51st (Ht) Div: presented ribbons. Sgt Downie 20140 & Cpl Taylor 20217 Pte Barclay 20223 being presented with Military Medal.	
AGENVILLERS	5		Company moved to AGENVILLERS.	
MAISON PONTHIEU	6		Company moved to MAISON PONTHIEU.	
HAUTE COUTE	7		Company moved to HAUTE COUTE.	
HERNICOURT	8		Company moved to HERNICOURT.	
DIEVAL	9		Company moved to DIEVAL	
CAUCOURT	10		Company moved to CAUCOURT.	
GUESTREVILLE	11		Company moved to GUESTREVILLE. 1 Officer and 27 OR proceeded to Brigade Hq to 2 Lieut AINSWORTH	
	12/21st		for purpose of wood cutting. Company in rest and training at GUESTREVILLE. LIEUT WES NAPIER left the Company on the 16th & took command of the 184th M.G. Company. LIEUT W.S.S. BROADBENT joined the Company on the 17th.	
BAJUS A.C.Q FREVIN CAPELLE	21st		Part of the Company (Lt Blackstock and 2/Lt McG and 64 OR) moves into billets at BAJUS taking 6 guns. Remainder took up positions in defence of dumps against hostile aircraft.	

WAR DIARY
INTELLIGENCE SUMMARY

Army Form C. 2118.

Place	Date	Hour	Summary of Events and Information	Remarks and references to Appendices
ACQ	21.1.		Disposition of Guns. 2 Guns each in defence of dumps at E.11 d.99 and E.11 d.12. ACQ. 1 gun each at E.17 a.8 and E.10 d.99 FREVIN CAPELLE. Map. sheet 51.C FRANCE.	
BAJUS	22-28		Detachment of Company at BAJUS in rest and training.	
	21		2/Lieut. F.J. ROWAN joined the Company from the BASE.	
	23		2/Lieut. R.R. McGREGOR and 29 O.R. joined the Company being Draft sent up from BASE	
	28		6 O.R. joined the Company from the BASE	

W S Marshead
Lieut for Capt.
COMDG. 153RD COY. M.G. CORPS

Vol 14/22

Confidential
War Diary
of
153rd Coy M.T. A.S.C.
from 1st March to 31 March 1917

(Vol 15)

Army Form C. 2118.

WAR DIARY
or
INTELLIGENCE SUMMARY.
(Erase heading not required.)

Instructions regarding War Diaries and Intelligence Summaries are contained in F. S. Regs., Part II. and the Staff Manual respectively. Title pages will be prepared in manuscript.

Place	Date	Hour	Summary of Events and Information	Remarks and references to Appendices
	1917 MARCH			
BATUS ACQ	1		Company HQ still at BATUS. Detachment at ACQ work our mountes for anti-aircraft work as at close of last month.	W/SB.
OURTON	2.		Company HQ and Section at BATUS removed to OURTON. W/R.	
	4		2/Lt MacGregor + N° 1 Coy. 7 Instructor in Practification of Aeroplanes at LATTRE St QUENTIN. W/MS	
	12		2/LT AINSWORTH and the wood-cutting party at FREVILLERS returned to Coy. at OURTON W/SB.	
BRAY	13		Company HQ Section at OURTON moves to BRAY, left OURTON 9.30 am, arrived BRAY 3 pm W/R.	
	13.		Detachment at ACQ relieves by 152 M.G. Coy a moves to BRAY. W/R.	
IN THE LINE ROCLINCOURT-ECURIE	16		Company relieves 154th M.G. Coy in the line ROCLINCOURT - ECURIE. W/R.	
			N°1 Section in reserve at ANZIN, N°2 holding centre sector, N°3 right sector, N°4 left sector W/R.	
			3000 rounds fires in indirect fire schemes W/SB.	
	17		2500 rounds fires in indirect fire schemes on German trenches and THELUS ROAD W/R. 2/LT ROBERTS joins the Company W/R.	
	18		6250 rounds fires in indirect fire schemes W/R.	
	19		6750 rounds fires in indirect fire schemes W/R.	
	20		Inter-sectional relief carried out as follows:- N°1 relieves N°4 in left sector, N°2 relieves N°3 in right sector, N°3 relieves N°1 at ANZIN, N°4 relieves N°2 in centre sector W/SB.	
	21		5000 rds fires in indirect fire schemes W/SB. 2 nos 9000 rounds fires in indirect fire schemes W/R	
	22		8 men from each Battn in the Brigade attached to the Company as working party. Work commenced on emplacements in RIPPERT AVENUE in preparation for coming offensive. W/MS.	
			6000 rounds fires in direct fire on KLEEMANN STELLUNG where Artillery have commenced to cut wire. W/R.	

[Signature]
Lt for Capt. MAJOR,
COMDG. 153RD COY. M.G. CORPS

Army Form C. 2118.

WAR DIARY
or
INTELLIGENCE SUMMARY.
(Erase heading not required.)

Instructions regarding War Diaries and Intelligence Summaries are contained in F.S. Regs., Part II. and the Staff Manual respectively. Title pages will be prepared in manuscript.

Place	Date	Hour	Summary of Events and Information	Remarks and references to Appendices
IN THE LINE	March 1917 23		10,000 rounds fires in indirect fire schemes, mostly on enemy wire. M.F.S	
	24		9000 rounds fires in indirect fire schemes mostly on enemy wire. M.F.S.	
	25		6500 rounds fires in indirect fire schemes. M.F.R. German aeroplane came under fire 9 gun in Western trench & believe it have been hit, as it turned back & planes down steeply & fell finally behind german lines. M.F.B. 200,000 rounds S.A.A. carries up from ROCLINCOURT & RIPPERT AVENUE. M.M.	
	26		8000 rounds fires in indirect fire schemes M.F.R. Private M.E. Leod, mortally wounded M.M. No. 20485	
	27		8500 rounds fires in indirect fire schemes M.F.R. 3 guns in ANZIN wounds near BETHUNE road for anti-aircraft work. M.F.R.	
	28		13 Emplacements in RIPPERT AVENUE now completed. M.M.	
	29		4950 rounds fires in indirect fire schemes M.F.R.	
	30		6250 rounds fires in indirect fire schemes M.M. Emplacements made in WESTERN trench in preparation for coming offensive.	
	31		Fire instruction on flanks given to 6th Black Watch in raid carried out by them on german front line M.F.R. 700 rounds fires in indirect fire scheme M.F.R.	

M.S. Westerbeek M.S. Coy.
COMDG. 153RD COY. M.G. CORPS.

CONFIDENTIAL

WAR DIARY

OF

153RD COMPANY MACHINE GUN CORPS

FROM 1st APRIL 1917 to 30th APRIL 1917

(VOLUME 33.)

Army Form C. 2118.

WAR DIARY
or
INTELLIGENCE SUMMARY
(Erase heading not required.)

Volume 33

Instructions regarding War Diaries and Intelligence Summaries are contained in F. S. Regs., Part II. and the Staff Manual respectively. Title pages will be prepared in manuscript.

Place	Date April 1917	Hour	Summary of Events and Information	Remarks and references to Appendices
ROCLINCOURT	1st		Company commenced the month in the line in positions the same as at the close of March. 5700 rounds fires in indirect fire schemes.	WSPB
	2nd		9700 rounds fires in indirect fire schemes mostly on enemy wire in front of KLEEMANN STELLUNG	WSPB
	3rd		5000 rounds fires in indirect fire schemes	WSPB
	4		5900 rounds fires in indirect fire schemes	WSPB
	5		3800 rounds fires in indirect fire schemes	WSPB
	6		6000 rounds fires in indirect fire schemes	GSPB
	7		6900 rounds fires in indirect fire schemes. The Battery Experiments for coming Offensive have finally cleared for action. Today is "X" day.	WSPB
	8		Company moved into Battle Emplacements, viz No 1 Section on extreme left in RIPPERT AVENUE, No 2 Section on No 1's right, No 4 on No 2's right and No 3 in WESTERN TRENCH. The Company plan of battle was as follows:- Overhead barrage fire zero to be fired from Zero until Zero plus 5 hours, varying from rapid to slow and intermittent fire. At Zero + 5 hours No 3 + 4 Sections were to advance to positions in the BROWN LINE	WSPB WSPB WSPB
	9	At about 2 am	2/Lt HASTWELL killed by shell fire	WSPB
		At Zero (i.e. 5:30am)	all guns opened barrage fire + continued fire until zero + 5 hours. Gradually lifting as the Infantry advanced. Total No. 9 rounds fires in barrage 93,500. Section 3 also had reserve orders to advance until about 3:30 pm. Lt MacNAUGHTON led this	WSPB WSPB

W.S. Broadhead Lieut.

T2134. Wt. W708—770. 500000. 4/15. Sir J.C. & S.

WAR DIARY

Army Form C. 2118.

— 2 —

Place	Date	Hour	Summary of Events and Information	Remarks and references to Appendices
ROCLINCOURT	April 1917 9.		In addition to positions in the BROWN line which had been vacated by the enemy, finally Lt MACNAUGHTON took up positions at B14 A 4.8 and B14 A 5.7 (see ROCLINCOURT map 6A. 1/10000) at 6 p.m. He then got into touch with the Canadians who had patrols in FARBUS Wood. On his right he walked a considerable way down the BROWN line trench but found it absolutely empty of either British or German troops. On returning to this point he found our Artillery were dropping shells into the Brown line trench and fearing he had advanced too far he withdrew his subsection about 30 yards to the 2nd Brown line trench. During this time 2Lt RIDGE had taken up position with his subsection at B19 B 3.9. 2/Lt RIDGE and Sgt HYND then went forward presumably to reconnoitre and were both sniped by the enemy & killed in TOMMY Trench.	bWB bSB bSB bSB bSB bSB
	10	6am	At 6 am on the 10th Lt MACNAUGHTON discovered strong parties of Germans had re-occupied the Brown line near B14 A 5.8 about 30 yards from the position of his guns. As he was totally unsupported by Infantry he carried out a further withdrawal of his subsection to B13 B 4.4. Where he was in touch with the 4th Gordon Highlanders.	bSB bSB
	11	4pm	At this time news came that the enemy had evacuated the Brown line between Tiries and Tommy Trenches (See ROCLINCOURT map within 6A 1/10000). Lt MACNAUGHTON then moved the 2 guns at B13 B 3.9 & with the infantry advanced again to the Brown line and mounted guns at B14 C 6.3 and B14 C 4.8. The other two guns he also advanced to	bSB bWB bWB

M McDonald Stewart
Lieut

WAR DIARY or INTELLIGENCE SUMMARY

Army Form C. 2118.

(Erase heading not required.)

Date	Hour	Summary of Events and Information	Remarks and references to Appendices
April 1917			
9		B14 A 4.8 and B14 A 5.7 WIB Section 3 rd relieves at 4.30 pm. WIB	
9	4.30	No 4 Section was withdrawn from Barrage line and advanced at 4.30 pm WIB Section moves 2/1 F.T. Rowan took up position at B19 D 2.5 and B19 D 2.8 and was in touch with 5th Gordon Highlanders on the right and 7th Argyle and Sutherland Highlanders on the left WIB.	
10	12/1 am	At midnight Section advanced and took up position in C1N trench at B20 A7.4 and B20 C 9.5. WIB Guns were in position by 1 am. WIB	
12	2 am	Section was relieved at 2 am. WIB	
12		Company was relieved and moved into huts at MARŒUIL. WIB	
13.04		Company resting and cleaning up at MARŒUIL. WIB	
15		Company moved into the line in the PAMPOUX Sector, relieving 6 guns 7 26th Coy and 8 guns 7 197th Coy. WIB. Section 3 and half of No 2 remained in reserve at ATHIES WIB. No 1 and half No 2 Section in front line position and No 4 in Support. WIB	
16		Half of No 2 moved from ATHIES into Support line. WIB No 4 Section fires 4000 rounds in moved fire. WIB	
17		No 3 Section relieves No 1 Section in front line. No 1 returns to ATHIES WIB	
18		[illegible] No 4 Section in front line and half of No 2 Section [illegible] WIB	
19		No 4 [illegible] and 1/2 No 2 in front line, No 3 and 1/2 No 2 in [illegible] WIB	

[signature]

WAR DIARY or INTELLIGENCE SUMMARY

Army Form C. 2118.

Place	Date	Hour	Summary of Events and Information	Remarks and references to Appendices
FAMPOUX	April 20	10pm	Six guns in front line relieved by 152 M.G. Coy. Guns relieved returned to Headquarters. The No. 3 Section and half of No. 2 Section moved up into Battle Position in Support line.	
	21		No. 3 Section and half No. 2 Section in Support Line.	
	22	7pm	All guns moved up into Battle Positions.	
	23.	4.45 am	8 guns opened barrage for 15 minutes.	
	23.	10 am	4 guns took up position in Old Jerusalem Trench. 16 guns eventually took up position in Hyderabad Redoubt. These guns owing to no infantry support have been thrown out. Guns were taken out of action at all being. The remains of guns were not part of the action at all. The remainder in Culling in Fampoux. in reserve	
		10 pm	4 guns from the barrage went forward to consolidate the position held by the infantry (i.e. the road running from the CHEMICAL WORKS to GAVRELLE)	
	24.		Company was relieved by 103 M.G. Co. & proceeded to billets in ARRAS.	
ARRAS	25.		Entrained at ARRAS for LIGNY-St-FLOCHEL & marched to MARQUAY	

W Maclies

Army Form C. 2118.

WAR DIARY
or
INTELLIGENCE SUMMARY.
(Erase heading not required.)

Instructions regarding War Diaries and Intelligence Summaries are contained in F. S. Regs., Part II. and the Staff Manual respectively. Title pages will be prepared in manuscript.

Place	Date	Hour	Summary of Events and Information	Remarks and references to Appendices
MARQUAY	26		Day spent in cleaning up.	
	27		Cleaning up continued.	
	28		Training commenced. 2 Lt. Young & 2 Lt. Smith joined the Battalion.	
	29		Sunday. Divine Service.	
	30		G.O.C. 51 Div. inspected all transport & Company training continued.	

Maclud.

Vol 16

Confidential

War Diary
-of-
153rd Company, Machine Gun Corps.

From 1st May 1917. To 31st May 1917.

(Volume 34.)

Army Form C. 2118.

WAR DIARY
or
INTELLIGENCE SUMMARY.
(Erase heading not required.)

153 Coy. M.G. Corps

Instructions regarding War Diaries and Intelligence Summaries are contained in F.S. Regs., Part II. and the Staff Manual respectively. Title pages will be prepared in manuscript.

Place	Date	Hour	Summary of Events and Information	Remarks and references to Appendices
MARQUAY.	MAY 1917.			
	1st		Company training (Open Country Warfare), 2nd Lt J.J. Rowan attached to the strength of the Company.	
	2nd		Company training continued.	
	3rd		Company training continued & testing new barrels & magazines on range.	
	4th		Company training continued. Brig. Gen. Campbell on handing over command of the Brigade said good-bye to Officers, N.C.O.s and men of the Coy.	
	5th		Company training continued.	
	6th		Divine Service. Lecture at TERNAS by the G.O.C. 61st (H) Div. to all officers and N.C.O.s on the use of Machine Guns in Attack and Defence, specially emphasising their use against counter attacks. Capt. H.P. Blackwood takes over command of the Company.	
	7th		Field Day, & practising attacks in conjunction with 1/5 Gordon Highlanders. Renewing & Guns on the range.	
	8th		Inspection of the Coy., Guns and gun equipment by the Coy. Offier.	

Army Form C. 2118.

WAR DIARY
or
INTELLIGENCE SUMMARY.
(Erase heading not required.)

153 soy M.G. Corps.

Instructions regarding War Diaries and Intelligence Summaries are contained in F. S. Regs., Part II. and the Staff Manual respectively. Title pages will be prepared in manuscript.

Place	Date	Hour	Summary of Events and Information	Remarks and references to Appendices
	MAY 1917			
MARQUAY	8th		No 2 Section relieved No 1 Section in anti-aircraft positions. 2 guns north of LINGY St FLOCHEL at T.23 c. & d. and 2 guns at ROLLECOURT; T27, c, o, 3. & T26, c, 9, 6.	
	9th		Inspection of transport by 4.O.c Brigade. 8 guns on tactical scheme in conjunction with 1/6 Black Watch, 4 guns on the range. 2nd Lt R.R. MacGregor struck off the strength of the company.	
	10th			
	11th		Tactical scheme. 4 guns on the range. Lewis sports in conjunction with 1/7 Gordon Highlanders.	
	12th		Company sports. No 2 Section relieved from anti-aircraft positions by 4 guns of 9th Division.	
ARRAS	13th		Company minus transport marches to LINGY St FLOCHEL and entrained for ARRAS. The transport, under transport officer, went by road.	
			Overhauling of guns, packing of limbers etc., preparatory to going into the lines.	

Army Form C. 2118.

WAR DIARY
or
INTELLIGENCE SUMMARY.
(Erase heading not required.)

153 Coy M.G. Corps

Place	Date	Hour	Summary of Events and Information	Remarks and references to Appendices
FAMPOUX	MAY 1917			
	14th		The company moved into the line in the FAMPOUX sector, relieving 16 guns of 11th Coy. 4th Division. Our guns took up the following positions:- 4 guns in front line, 4 guns in L Quarry, and 6 guns in FAMPOUX. German shelling was exceedingly accurate, owing to which Coy. H.Q. moved from FAMPOUX to Sunken Rd. N. of newly-cut gunpits.	
	15th		The disposition of guns was changed, and went forward as follows:- 4 guns in front line, 2 in "L" Quarry, 2 in gun pits N. of FAMPOUX and 8 guns in FAMPOUX in reserve. Our guns fired 7500 rounds on a barrage from I.9.a.55. to I.15.a.3.9. in support of Brigade counter attack at 9.30 AM. O.C. left section reported that at 1 am left flank of 9.30 am counter attack held up in town, and our attacking troops were still up in position with two M/G. sections. Later he reported that he was in position with two guns on left flank, 2 guns completed to relieve from CROOK.	
	16th		guns on right flank, 2 guns reported our attack which followed and came at 5.5 am. He occupied positions.	
	17th	At 7.30 pm	had failed to take its objective. He occupied position. 2 guns in KUBA Hot N. of CROOK. 2 guns in trench connecting CROOK and CROW as in position. The two guns which had moved from CROOK when attacked by hostile infantry having suffered were compelled to abandon tripods and belts. Guns	

A5834 Wt. W.4973/M687 750,000 8/16 D.D.&L.Ltd Forms/C.2118/13

WAR DIARY or INTELLIGENCE SUMMARY

Army Form C. 2118.

153 Army Bde. R.G.A.

Place	Date	Hour	Summary of Events and Information	Remarks and references to Appendices
FAMPOUX	MAY 1917 17th		The 2 guns in CUSHION remained in action. Orders for their withdrawal were dispatched at 10 a.m. 20 Division on our left advanced their sector. The two missing guns from Chemical Works are reported by infantry in this area to have done good execution before being overrun by hostile attack. Hostile barrage was very heavy on our line of ROEUX - GAVRELLE Road. Hostile working parties are reported by our personnel to have advanced to our front line before bombardment on Chemical Works opened. 2nd Lt. G.A. Eadie to be temp. Lieut, date 16.5.17.	AM
	18th		Between 8 & 9 a.m. hostile artillery bombardment became very heavy. Between 8 a.m. and 9 a.m. a hostile aeroplane was brought down at I.7.d.2.3. by our machine gun fire.	AM
	19th		Hostile artillery very quiet. Enemy appear to lack initiative in pushing on.	AM
	20th		Slight shelling through the night in the vicinity of "L" Quarry sh. I.7.d.9.3. Our aircraft were fired upon by enemy machine guns with no apparent result. Our a.a. guns fired 500 rds. gm	AM
	21st			
	22nd		Aerial activity of our machines was very great arriving late afternoon and evening. Staking about 11 p.m. cross roads west end of FAMPOUX were frequently shelled. Sth A.S.m. 4.5. g.m. guns	AM

A5834 Wt. W4973/M687 750,000 8/16 D. D. & L. Ltd. Forms/C.2118/13.

WAR DIARY or INTELLIGENCE SUMMARY

Army Form C. 2118.

(Erase heading not required.)

153 Coy M.G. Corps

Place	Date	Hour	Summary of Events and Information	Remarks and references to Appendices
	MAY 1917			
FAMPOUX	22nd		3pm - 6pm enemy shelled vicinity of "L" Quarry. CAMEL and CUBA and CHEMICAL WORKS were also shelled 5pm	
	23rd		from the road up to CUBA. A troop of hostile planes crossed our line about 9.45pm. They were fired on by our A.A. guns. Enemy fire no sooner out on hostile trenches 3000 rounds were fired 8pm	
	24th		Heavy enemy shelling on gun pits H.17.C.3.5. 4000 rounds fired in indirect fire schemes on enemy communication trench. Our A.A. guns fired 4500 rounds. Coy relieved by 152 Coy M.G.C. and marched to billets in ARRAS. 8pm	
ARRAS	25th		Cleaning up. 8pm	
	26th		Cleaning guns and equipment. Inspection by C.O. of army gun.	
	27th		Inspection by the G.O.C. 2nd Lt W.H. Hampson joined the coy. 8th	
	28th		Lt A.J. Richards & 2nd Lt A.B. Riddle joined & taken on the strength of the coy. 8pm	

Army Form C. 2118.

WAR DIARY
or
INTELLIGENCE SUMMARY.
(Erase heading not required.)

153rd Coy M.G Corps

Instructions regarding War Diaries and Intelligence Summaries are contained in F. S. Regs., Part II. and the Staff Manual respectively. Title pages will be prepared in manuscript.

Place	Date	Hour	Summary of Events and Information	Remarks and references to Appendices
ARRAS.	MAY 1917			
	29th		The Coy moved back by motor bus to MARQUAY.	
MARQUAY.	30th		Company training.	
	31st		Coy training.	

[signature]
Capt.
COMDG. 153RD COY. M.G. CORPS.

Confidential

War Diary
- of -

153rd Company, Machine Gun Corps.

From 1st June 1917 to 30th June 1917.

(Volume 35)

Army Form C.2...

WAR DIARY
or
INTELLIGENCE SUMMARY.
(Erase heading not required.)

153rd Company Machine Gun Corps

Instructions regarding War Diaries and Intelligence Summaries are contained in F.S. Regs., Part II and the Staff Manual respectively. Title pages will be prepared in manuscript.

Place	Date	Hour	Summary of Events and Information	Remarks and references to Appendices
	June 1917			
MARQUAY	1st		Company Training and Route March. JMW	
Do.	2nd		Divine Service. Draft of 14 O.R's taken on Strength of the Company. JMW	
Do.	3rd		Company marched to billets in BOYAVAL. 2nd Lieut J.R.W. Mitchell struck off Strength of Company. JMW	
BOYAVAL	4th		Company marched to billets in ERNY-ST-JULIEN. JMW	
ERNY-ST-JULIEN	5th		Parades + Inspections. 2nd Lieut Roberts struck off Strength. JMW	
Do.	6th		Company marched to billets in WISERNES. JMW	
WISERNES	7th		Company marched to billets in ZUDROVE (nr SERQUES). JMW	
ZUDROVE	8th		Reveille at 4:30 A.M. Nos 1+2 Sections firing on short range in ULAROUS at Q.16.9 during morning. Nos 3 + 4 Sections Do. during afternoon. Recreational training during evening. Draft of 26 O.R. from Base Depot. JMW	
Do.	9th		Divine Service. JMW	
Do.	10th		Company Training continued (Rough ground drill, use of tripod &c). Rifle + Revolver practice on Short Range. Physical training. JMW	
Do.	11th		Company training continued. (Action from limbers &c). 2/Lt W.B. Savage and 2/Lt A.T. Seager from Base Depot taken on Strength. JMW	

WAR DIARY
or
INTELLIGENCE SUMMARY.
(Erase heading not required.)

Army Form C.2118

153rd Company Machine Gun Corps

Instructions regarding War Diaries and Intelligence Summaries are contained in F. S. Regs., Part II. and the Staff Manual respectively. Title pages will be prepared in manuscript.

Place	Date	Hour	Summary of Events and Information	Remarks and references to Appendices
	June 1917			
LUDROVE	12th		Saw Seventi Company Tactical Scheme during forenoon in Brigade Training Area. — 2 O.Rs from Base Depot taken on strength.	
Do	13		Company Shooting Competition on short range (Machine Gun Rifle & Revolver).	
Do	14		Company Drill, Gas Drill & Musical Training. — 1 O.R. taken on strength.	
Do	15th		Inspection of Guns, Harness and Rifles by Divisional Armourer Sergeant. Company training continued. — 2/Lt H. Roberts rejoined from Hospital.	
Do	16th		Divine Service.	
Do	17		Company firing on Long Range ("A" Range Telegraph Training area) 5000 rounds per section fired. — 2nd Lieut Richards and Lieut Giles transferred to 189th Company.	
Do	18th		Company Training continued (Mechanism, Gun Drill, Bayonet Drill & Training on Short Range). Divisional Horse Show. 2nd Prize for Limber Transport and 3rd prize for Light Draft won by Company.	
Do	19th		Packing of Limbers preparatory to move. 10 other ranks returned to Base Depot preparatory to proceeding to POPERINGHE area. Transport seconded to Lord Leatington proceeded by road to POPERINGHE.	
Do	20th		Company moves & entrained for WATTEN and entrained for ESQUIMPANT A30.c.9.5 (Sheet 28 N.E.)	
POPERINGHE	21st		Marched to ESQUIMPANT A30.c.9.5 (Sheet 28 N.E.)	

Army Form C.2118.

WAR DIARY
or
INTELLIGENCE SUMMARY.

(Erase heading not required)

153rd Company Machine Gun Corps

Instructions regarding War Diaries and Intelligence Summaries are contained in F.S. Regs., Part II. and the Staff Manual respectively. Title pages will be prepared in manuscript.

Place	Date	Hour	Summary of Events and Information	Remarks and references to Appendices
"E" CAMP	June 1917 22nd		Overhauling and cleaning of Guns, Equipment etc, preparatory to going into the line. — Nos 3 & 4 Sections moved to Huts near Transport lines on A.28.c.5.4. Sm	
Do	23rd		Nos 1 and 2 Sections moved into the line and relieved 8 guns of the 117th Company Machine Gun Corps. — No 1 Section occupied the positions in C.20.c.b.3; C.20.d.9.1; and C.21.a.8.3. Two guns of No 1 Section occupied positions in C.19.b.6.5, and was under supervision of O.C. No 2 Section. — Two 4 guns of No 2 Section took over the positions in C.20.a.05.35 C.14.c.25.35, C.14.c.25.40, and C.14.d.10.05. Headquarters situated in CANAL BANK Jm	
IN LINE	24th		Considerable Artillery Activity during the day most of the gun positions being heavily shelled. O.C. No 1 Section reports that a considerable amount of Tear shells were fired by enemy between 2am and 3am. The trench between Guns Dousbons to MC.25.35 and C.14.c.25.40 was considerably damaged by Enemy Artillery fire. Sm	
Do	25th		Clifford Towers + Jock's Farm were shelled by Enemy Artillery during the night. The position in C.20.a.05.35 was damaged by Artillery	

Army Form C. 2118.

WAR DIARY
or
INTELLIGENCE SUMMARY.

(Erase heading not required.)

153rd Company, Machine Gun Corps

Instructions regarding War Diaries and Intelligence Summaries are contained in F. S. Regs., Part II. and the Staff Manual respectively. Title pages will be prepared in manuscript.

Place	Date	Hour	Summary of Events and Information	Remarks and references to Appendices
	June 1917			
INLINE	25th	(cont)	fire during the day. A quantity of trench stores were also damaged at this position. No 65866 Private G. L. Skipp, No 2 Section slightly wounded. (Remained on duty). DM	
Do	26th		Enemy's Artillery was active during the period. D.O. No 1 Section reports an abnormal number of "dud" shells fell near Loch Farm. DM	
Do	27th		Considerable Artillery shelling during the day. One gun of No 1 Section mounted near Loch Farm was hit by a small piece of shrapnel. An alternative emplacement near CLIFFORD TOWERS (B21/a 9.3) was completed by No 1 Section. The CANAL BANK was heavily shelled during the forenoon. No 3 Section moved into this line and occupied dug-outs in Canal Bank. DM	
Do	28th		Hostile Artillery was less active during this night, but increased somewhat during the day. The Trench between C14 c 25.40 and C14 c 35.35 was badly damaged by shell fire. 250 rounds were fired at enemy aircraft. No 291604 Private Arthur J. (attached from 117th Brigade M.G.C.) killed in action. 20.50 L/Cpl Bremner J. and 39237 Pte Walker A. wounded. DM	

Army Form C. 2118.

WAR DIARY
or
INTELLIGENCE SUMMARY.

(Erase heading not required.)

153rd Company Machine Gun Corps

Place	Date	Hour	Summary of Events and Information	Remarks and references to Appendices
IN LINE	June 1917 29th		Hostile Artillery was very active during the period. The Gun positions of No 3 Section were intermittently shelled during the day. N.L. No 3 Section reports a heavy enemy bombardment on left at 11.30 p.m. The Canal Bank was again heavily shelled during the evening. There was considerable hostile aerial activity. No 4 Section moved into the line and relieved No 2 Section. No 2 Section moved into Bearwood Lines A.28.C.5.4. 97519 Private Clements H. No 3 Section, died of wounds. 8m	
	30th		No 4 Section Emplacements were heavily shelled between 2 a.m. and 4 a.m. Several direct hits were obtained at the junction of 'K' LINE and HALIFAX ROAD. An alternative position was completed in NORTH STREET by No 3 Section. Enemy's Artillery were less active during the remainder of the day. 81858 Private H Watters and 91542 Private W Brown killed in action. 28939 Private T. Torrance wounded (Remained on duty) sm	

Signature
COMDG. 153rd COY. M.G. CORPS

Vol 18

CONFIDENTIAL
No 81(A)
HIGHLAND
DIVISION.

Confidential

War Diary

153rd Coy Machine Gun Corps

From 1st July 1917 to 31st July 1917

Volume 36

WAR DIARY
or
INTELLIGENCE SUMMARY.
(Erase heading not required.)

Army Form C. 2118.

153d Coy M.G. Corps

Place	Date	Hour	Summary of Events and Information	Remarks and references to Appendices
In the Line	1st		Hostile Artillery has active during the day. Shelled during the in "X" Lyne and Lifford Lines. were heavily shelled during the afternoon and evening	M
	2nd		All gun emplacements were intermittently shelled during the period. 250 rounds were fired on enemy aircraft. 2nd Lt Rogers and ten men of No 2 Section relieved 10 men of No 1. in reserve at Canal Bank.	M
	3rd		Enemy shelling less intense than on previous days. Hermans aeroplanes were active. We fired 400 rounds on hostile aircraft	M
	4.		Artillery very quiet. Several shells fell near our forward gun emplacements. Hostile aircraft were again active. Our guns fired 3500 rounds	M
	5th		Coy relieved by 165 2nd Coy. Moved back to "D" Camp A. 30 central.	M

WAR DIARY
or
INTELLIGENCE SUMMARY.
(Erase heading not required.)

Army Form C. 2118.

Volume 36

Place	Date	Hour	Summary of Events and Information	Remarks and references to Appendices
ST. MAMELIN			153 Bdy 4th A. Bde/fo	
	July 1917.			
	6th		Bdy moved by motor buses from "D" camp to St Mamelin	Mn
	7th		General clean up and tour of practice trenches	Mn
	8th		Church parade. 2nd Lt W.B. Savage joined Bde strength of the Bdy. Extract from Army List 2nd Lt H. Ainsworth promoted 2nd/Lt Lieut.	Mn
	9th		Bdy training. Inspection by C.O. of guns and all gun equipment. Also lecture to officers, N.C.O.s, & men on Map reading	Mn
	10th		Bdy Drill. Extract from Army List 2nd Lt R.C. Barlow promoted Lieut.	Mn
	11th		Route march. Tour of practice trenches and artillery formations on practice.	Mn
	12th		Company training	Mn
	13th		Brigade practice attack	Mn
	14th		Physical exercise and kilect inspection by C.O.	Mn
	15th		Church parade	Mn
	16th		Practice of barrage scheme on Brigade training area	Mn
	17th		do do	Mn

WAR DIARY
or
INTELLIGENCE SUMMARY.
(Erase heading not required.)

Army Form C. 2118.

Place	Date	Hour	Summary of Events and Information	Remarks and references to Appendices
ST MOMELIN	July 1917		153 Coy M.G. Corps	
	18th		Brigade practice attack, mapreading and report writing	M
	19th		do	M
	20th		do	M
	21st		Gun cleaning and inspection of guns and equipment	M
	22nd		Church parade	M
	23rd		Miscellaneous training map reading report writing etc.	M
	24th		Coy. moved by motor buses from St Momelin to Windmill Camp A.17.d. Transport moved by road	M
Wind mill Camp			under transport officer	M
	25th		Rest and generally cleaning up.	M
	26th		Coy training.	M
	27th		Gun and Box respirator drill.	M
	28th		Building of open emplacements.	M
	29th		Packing of limbers preparatory to moving into line. Coy left Windmill Camp A.17.d. 9pm., marching via	M

WAR DIARY
INTELLIGENCE SUMMARY

Army Form C. 2118.

Place	Date	Hour	Summary of Events and Information	Remarks and references to Appendices
	July 1917			
	29th		RUM ROAD to Canal Bank. Hd. Qrs. & Nos 3 & 4 Sections going on to battle positions. 153 Coy M.G. Corps Nos 1 & 2 Sections having dumped their Guns and equipment, left themin charge of No.1 and returned to transport lines, Windmill Camp.	
	30th		During the night enemy shelled x heavily with gas shells. 7.30 pm No 2 Sect left transport lines. 2nd Lt H Roberts and two gun teams, 2nd Lt A.T. Seager and two gun teams reporting to O's & /5 Gordon Hrs & /6 Black Watch respectively. 8.30 pm 3 & 4 Sections moved from Canal Bank to their rendezvous Highland Farm, thence to Barrage positions 9 & 10 boy. Hd. Qrs. moved to Lancashire Farm; battle Hd. Qrs. No 2 Sect. Zero 3.50 am. Two guns attached to each battalion went forwards with attacking waves, to consolidate BLUE and BLACK lines. Remaining eight guns did barrage work from n positions taken up at 9 am in CANE AVE.	

JMoody Lt in capt-
COMDG. 153rd COY. M.G. CORPS

Vol 19

Confidential

War Diary

— of —

153rd Company, Machine Gun Corps.

From 1st August 1917 to 31st August 1917.

Volume 37

Army Form C. 2118.

WAR DIARY
or
INTELLIGENCE SUMMARY.
(Erase heading not required).

Volume 387

Place	Date	Hour	Summary of Events and Information	Remarks and references to Appendices
In the line	1st August 1917.		153 Coy machine guns taken over by 154th Coy. Coy in line. Relieved. Relief marched back independently to Siege Camp, arriving about 4 am on the morning of the 2nd. Total casualties during tour of the line 1 Officer (2Lt H. Roberts) and 21 O.R.s.	A/3.
SIEGE CAMP.	2nd		General clean up of guns, rifles, equipment and clothing. Inspection by O.C. Coy of all guns, rifles, equipment and kits.	A/3.
	3rd			A/3.
"Z" CAMP ST JAN TER BIEZEN	4th 5th		Coy moved from Siege Camp at 1.55 pm to "Z" Camp St Jan Ter Biezen, arriving there about 5.30 pm. Church Parade.	A/3. A/3.
BIEZEN	6th		Inspection of Coy by O.C. 10 am. Inspection of rifles and equipment.	A/3.
	7th	9am	Coy training. Officers and N.C.O.s advanced training under O.C. Coy. 2Lt H.A. Ainsworth struck off the	A/3.

WAR DIARY
or
INTELLIGENCE SUMMARY.
(Erase heading not required.)

Army Form C. 2118.

Place	Date	Hour	Summary of Events and Information	Remarks and references to Appendices
ST. JAN TER.	7th		Strength of the Company, transferred to U.K.	A/3.
	8th		Tactical scheme, action from Pack Transport.	A/3.
BIEZEN.	9th		Action from pack transport. Officers and N.C.O's advanced training under O.C. Coy.	A/3.
	10th		Musketry. Officers and N.C.O's lecture by M.O.C. Brigade action from limbers and action from packs.	A/3.
	11th		Inspection of kits, equipment, rifles, guns and gear. Mechanism for O.Rs attached from battalions.	A/3.
	12th		Church parades arrival of 15 O.Rs from base.	A/3.
	13th		Tactical scheme, action from packs and artillery formation	A/3.
	14th		Discrimination and recognition of targets, miscellaneous training under O.C. Coy.	A/3.
	15th		Officers and N.C.O's advanced training Officers and N.C.O's map reading	A/3.
	16th		Range. 1000 rounds per gun fired	A/3.
			Miscellaneous training Officers and N.C.O's map reading	A/3.
	17th		Tactical scheme, use of compass under O.C. and use of ground and court, instruction	A/3.

Army Form C. 2118.

WAR DIARY
or
INTELLIGENCE SUMMARY.
(Erase heading not required.)

Instructions regarding War Diaries and Intelligence Summaries are contained in F. S. Regs., Part II. and the Staff Manual respectively. Title pages will be prepared in manuscript.

Place	Date	Hour	Summary of Events and Information	Remarks and references to Appendices
	August 1917.			
ST JAN TER.	18th		Range. 1000 rounds pergun fired.	O.B.
	19th		Church parade afternoon baths. Two ORs transferred from 152 Coy	O.B.
BIEZEN.	20th		Miscellaneous training; Officers and N.C.O's instruction on Lewis light Gun. Afternoon: Coy on shot range.	O.B.
	21st		Miscellaneous training; No 5 1 and 2 sec of gun and tripod slings.	O.B.
	22nd		Musketry. Nos 1 and 2 instruction in indirect fire	O.B.
			Kit inspection by O.C. Coy.	
	23rd		Miscellaneous training, action from packs. afternoon Advanced training	O.B.
	24th		Tactical scheme. feature by C.O. to officers + NCOs Advanced flank and rear guards.	O.B.
	25th		Inspection of Kits, guns and rifles	O.B.
	26th		Church parade. Extract from Bde Routine Orders 20118 Sgt Killick J. and 20489 Sgt Stephen I.G. awarded the military Medal for gallantry displays on the 31st July	O.B.

2353 Wt. W2544/1454 700,000 5/15 D. D. & L. A.D.S.S. Forms/C 2118.

Army Form C. 2118.

WAR DIARY
or
INTELLIGENCE SUMMARY.
(Erase heading not required.)

Place	Date	Hour	Summary of Events and Information	Remarks and references to Appendices
ST JAN TER.	August 1917		153 Coy Machine Gun Corps.	
	26th		and 1st August. 16 ORs attached (tempy) from 1/5 London Highrs.	A/3.
	27th		Whole Coy inspected by G.O.C. Division.	A/3.
BIEZEN.	28th		Range: 1000 rounds per gun fired.	A/3.
	29th		Packing of limbers etc: moving to forward area. Afternoon: baths.	A/3.
SIEGE CAMP	30th		Coy. moved from "Z" Camp to SIEGE CAMP. arriving at 12 noon	A/3.
"	31st		2 guns with 4/7 London Highlanders in defence scheme; remainder Tactical exercise; Consolidation.	A/3.

A Boyer Lt & Capt.
COMDG. 153RD COY. M.G. CORPS.

Vol 20

Confidential

War Diary
—of—

153rd Company, Machine Gun Corps.

From 1st Sept 1917 to 31st Sept 1917.

(Volume 38.)

Army Form C. 2118.

WAR DIARY
or
INTELLIGENCE SUMMARY.
(Erase heading not required.) N'Blaaret 38

Instructions regarding War Diaries and Intelligence Summaries are contained in F. S. Regs., Part II. and the Staff Manual respectively. Title pages will be prepared in manuscript.

Place	Date	Hour	Summary of Events and Information	Remarks and references to Appendices
SIEGE CAMP	1.9.17		Inspection of gun equipment, rifles, and ammunition by O.C. Company	A.3
	2.9.17		Church parade. - 2/Lieut W.B. SAVAGE reported from Base Depot	A.3
	3.9.17		Tactical exercise in conjunction with infantry, 2 guns attached to each Battalion in the Brigade. Remaining 8 guns miscellaneous training. -	A.3
	4.9.17		Consolidation of shell craters. 8 guns attached to Battalions for tactical exercise. -	A.3
	5.9.17		Tactical exercises and miscellaneous training. -	A.3
	6.9.17		Tactical exercises and miscellaneous training. -	A.3
MENIN QUE	7.9.17		Left SIEGE CAMP at 8 a.m. and proceeded to the village of MENIN QUE. Arrived at billets at 2 p.m. - Transport of Company remained at WINDMILL CAMP. -	A.3
"	8.9.17		Reconnoitred Field Firing Range with Company Officers. Range was situated about 6 miles from billets. - Preparing guns and ammunition for firing next day. -	A.3
	9.9.17		Company marched to range at 6 a.m. Guns & being conveyed by	

2333 Wt. W2511/1454 700,000 5/15 D. D. & L. A.D.S.S./Forms/C. 2118.

Army Form C. 2118.

WAR DIARY
or
INTELLIGENCE SUMMARY.
(Erase heading not required.)

Instructions regarding War Diaries and Intelligence Summaries are contained in F.S. Regs., Part II. and the Staff Manual respectively. Title pages will be prepared in manuscript.

Place	Date	Hour	Summary of Events and Information	Remarks and references to Appendices
MENTQUE	9.9.17		motor lorry. Carried out long range firing practices. Returned to billets at 2 p.m.	A/5
	10.9.17		Range firing during morning. Left MENTQUE at 3 p.m. by motor lorry.	A/5
SIEGE CAMP	11.9.17		Arrived SIEGE CAMP 8 p.m.	A/5
	12.9.17		Company moved into line relieving the 151st M.G. Company NE of YPRES. 8 guns in "Pill boxes" covering our outpost line and 8 guns in reserve on the CANAL BANK. Relief completed without casualties.	A/5
	13.9.17		Heavy enemy shelling about 10.30 a.m. this east of our billets mounted. Casualties nil. 6 guns of 253 M.G. Company were attached to this Coy.	A/5
	14.9.17		450 rounds fired in conjunction with artillery shoot at enemy working parties. 150 rounds fired at enemy aircraft. Construction of position continued. One gun moved from CANAL BANK into a post on outpost line at U.30.a.5.8. One gun to outskirts PHEASNT TRENCH this relief gun to form out post in conjunction with an "Chinese attack" on morning of 15th.	A/5
WHITE HOUSE				

Army Form C. 2118.

WAR DIARY
or
INTELLIGENCE SUMMARY.
(Erase heading not required.)

Instructions regarding War Diaries and Intelligence Summaries are contained in F. S. Regs., Part II. and the Staff Manual respectively. Title pages will be prepared in manuscript.

Place	Date	Hour	Summary of Events and Information	Remarks and references to Appendices
IN THE LINE	15.9.17		During night of 14/15th 2000 rounds fired on tracks and strong points	AB
	15.9.17	10 am	During "CHINESE ATTACK" the two guns in the outpost fired 3000 rounds	AB
		10 am	direct on Targets.	
		10-11 pm	3000 rounds fired by Barrage guns during Artillery Shoot on tracks and strong points	
			Construction of emplacements for Barrage Guns.	
	16.9.17	4 pm	Harassing fire carried out at intervals during night 15/16th. 5000 rds fired in 10 groupers with Artillery shoot at 5 am. Construction of Barrage emplacements and carrying of ammunition to Barrage position. 2 Guns in the outpost line moved back to the CANAL BANK - Casualties 3 O.Rs killed, 10 O.R. wounded, caused by a direct hit on a shelter.	AB
	17.9.17		During night 16/17th 11000 fired on ROSE HOUSE and surrounding area. 2nd & guns in the line were relieved by 1st & guns from the CANAL BANK. Construction of emplacements. Casualties 2 O.Rs killed 1 O.R. wounded.	AB

Army Form C. 2118.

WAR DIARY
or
INTELLIGENCE SUMMARY.
(Erase heading not required.)

Instructions regarding War Diaries and Intelligence Summaries are contained in F. S. Regs. Part II. and the Staff Manual respectively. Title pages will be prepared in manuscript.

Place	Date	Hour	Summary of Events and Information	Remarks and references to Appendices
IN THE LINE	18.9.17		Harassing fire carried out during night. Casualties nil.	
	19.9.17		During night 18/19th Barrage gun positions were completed. Flash obs & gun net the line and moved over to Barrage positions at N.29.c.4.5. The 8 guns on the CANAL BANK moved back by teams to camps N.E. of POPERINGHE.	AB.
	20.9.17		The 8 Barrage guns were in position and ready to fire at 3 new line concrete Machine Gun Emplacements about 20 yards from front position was consolidated for Lett filling. Guns commenced firing at 5.40 a.m. (zero hour) and continued for 4 minutes on first line of barrage, then lifted to second line and continued for 30 minutes, then 37 minutes about for 35 minutes. during this time was then lifted to 505 line and continued for 35 minutes. during this time 29,000 rounds were fired. During the remainder of day 10,000 rounds were fired intermittently and when called for on the Jett & from Wt 6.30 p.m. 2 Guns from Barrage positions were taken forward to WHITE HOUSE as it was thought the situation demanded it. Casualties during 20th September: 1 O.R. killed. 2 O.R. died of wounds. 9 O.Rs wounded. The Maj-	Sundown

Army Form C. 2118.

WAR DIARY
or
INTELLIGENCE SUMMARY.
(Erase heading not required.)

Instructions regarding War Diaries and Intelligence Summaries are contained in F. S. Regs., Part II. and the Staff Manual respectively. Title pages will be prepared in manuscript.

Place	Date	Hour	Summary of Events and Information	Remarks and references to Appendices
IN THE LINE	20.9.17		Company at X Camp resting.	A/B
	21.9.17		The 2 guns at WHITE HOUSE now moved back to Barrage position - Guns now withdrawn from Barrage positions and moved back to X Camp by Motor bus. Half Company at X Camp cleaning of guns and spare.	A/B
X Camp	22.9.17		Inspection of guns ammunition rifles etc by C.O.	A/B
	23.9.17		Church Services	A/B
	24.9.17		Cleaning of equipment. Recreational games. Capt H.F. Blackwood transferred to 30th Division at 9m B.O.	A/B
	25.9.17		Arms Drill. Inspection of S.B. Respirators and Box Helmet. Recreational games	A/B
	26.9.17		Squad Drill, Musketry, Lewis Drill. Lecture to Officers and N.C.O.'s on Maps reading and use of Prismatic Compass.	A/B
	27.9.17		1 Officer and 40 O.Rs moved by train from POPERINGHE to BAPAUME area as billeting party. Company training continued	A/B
	28.9.17		Company preparing to move. Company paraded at 5.15 p.m. and marched to PROVEN. Entrained and left at 9.15 p.m.	A/B

Army Form C. 2118.

WAR DIARY
or
INTELLIGENCE SUMMARY.
(Erase heading not required.)

Place	Date	Hour	Summary of Events and Information	Remarks and references to Appendices
	29.9.17		Arrived at BAPAUME at 8.30 a.m. Detrained and marched to Camp at GOMIECOURT. - Arrived at 12 noon.	A/3
GOMIECOURT	30.9.17		Church Service. CAPT. C.H. ROSE took over command of Company.	A/3

A. Bryce Lieut for Capt.
COMDG. 157th COY. M.G. CORPS

Confidential

War Diary
— of —

153rd Company, Machine Gun Corps.

From 1st Oct, 1917 to 31st Oct, 1917.

(Volume 9)

WAR DIARY
or
INTELLIGENCE SUMMARY.

Army Form C. 2118.

Volume 39

Place	Date	Hour	Summary of Events and Information	Remarks and references to Appendices
GOMMECOURT	October 1917 1st		Company Parades. Musketry. Gun Drill	A/S
	2nd		Arm Drill. Miscellaneous training	A/S
	3rd		Gun Clearing. Mechanism, Stoppages and Musketry	A/S
Coy H.Q. in Line S.E. of ARRAS	4th		Reveille 5 am. Nos 1, 2 and 3 Sections proceeded to line by Motor Bus. Relieved the 149th Machine Gun Company in the CHERISY SECTOR. Relief complete 2 p.m. No casualties. No 4 Section proceeded by Motor Bus to reserve position.	A/S
(CHERISY SECTOR)	5th		Very quiet on front. Majority of positions excellent. Deep Dug-outs for men. Trenches in good condition.	A/S
	6th		Day quiet. 7000 rounds fired on tracks and dumps during night 6/7th.	A/S
	7th		Day quiet. 7500 rounds expended in night firing	A/S
	8th		Operations:- 3700 rounds indirect fire. Day Quiet. 2/Lt HAMPSON in H. admitted to Hospital sick	A/S
	9th		4000 rounds fired in conjunction with Artillery shoot. No enemy retaliation.	A/S

Army Form C. 2118.

WAR DIARY
or
INTELLIGENCE SUMMARY.

(Erase heading not required.)

Instructions regarding War Diaries and Intelligence Summaries are contained in F. S. Regs., Part II. and the Staff Manual respectively. Title pages will be prepared in manuscript.

Place	Date	Hour	Summary of Events and Information	Remarks and references to Appendices
COY. HDQRS.	9th	(not clear)	Nos 3 + 4 Sections relieved Nos 1 + 2 Sections during daylight.	Q/3
IN LINE SE.	10th		3,500 rounds fired on special targets during the night	Q/3
of ARRAS	11th		1,500 rounds fired during night 11/12th. 250 rounds fired on enemy working	Q/3
(CHERISY	12th		party during day; enemy retaliated with M. G. fire.	Q/3
SECTOR)	13th		1,250 rounds fired on tracks during night 12/13th	Q/3
	14th		Day quiet. 5000 rounds expended during night 13/14th	Q/3
			4000 rounds fired in conjunction with "Gas Projectile" shoot	Q/3
			2,000 rounds fired on tracks during night 14/15th	
	15th		5,500 rounds fired on tracks behind FONTAINE-LES-CROISILLES, enemy retaliated with Artillery. No damage.	Q/3
MERCATEL	16th		The Company were relieved during day of 16th by the 152nd M.G. Company. Relief completed at 3 p.m. Company marched back to Camp 1 mile N. of MERCATEL. Accommodation—Huts. Casualties during period in trenches - NIL	Q/3
	17th		Cleaning of Equipment, Guns, Rifles etc.—	Q/3
	18th		Gun and Squad Drill.— Inspection of Guns etc. by C.O.	Q/3

Army Form C. 2118.

WAR DIARY
or
INTELLIGENCE SUMMARY.
(Erase heading not required.)

Instructions regarding War Diaries and Intelligence Summaries are contained in F. S. Regs., Part II. and the Staff Manual respectively. Title pages will be prepared in manuscript.

Place	Date	Hour	Summary of Events and Information	Remarks and references to Appendices
MERCATEL	19th		Squad Drill, S.B. Respirators and Smoke Helmet Drill, Gun Laying Recreational Games.	A/3
	20th		Inspection by an American Divisional General. Following awards notified. LIEUT IN D MACNAUGHTON, Military Cross. Sgt DUNCAN D.C.M. L/Cpls FORSTER & SKIPP Military Medal.	A/3
	21st		Church Parade. + OR's reinforcements.	A/3
	22nd		Saluting Drill, Gun Drill Mechanisms and gun cleaning, Recreational Games and map reading	A/3
	23rd		Musketry, short fronts Gun Drill, Immediate Action and Belt filling Recreational Games Arm Drill Indication and recognition of Targets.	A/3
	24th		Immediate Action and Gun Drill, Laying out of lines of fire. -	A/3
	25th		Squad and Arm Drill, Advanced training S.B. Respirators and Smoke Helmet Drill, Recreational Games.	A/3
	26th		Musketry and Knobel practices, Advanced training and recreational Games.	A/3
	27th		Inspection by D.M.G.O.	A/3

Army Form C. 2118.

WAR DIARY
or
INTELLIGENCE SUMMARY.
(Erase heading not required.)

Instructions regarding War Diaries and Intelligence Summaries are contained in F. S. Regs., Part II. and the Staff Manual respectively. Title pages will be prepared in manuscript.

Place	Date	Hour	Summary of Events and Information	Remarks and references to Appendices
NANQUETIN	28th		Company moved by road to the village of NANQUETIN. Left Camp at MERCATEL at 9am. Arrived in NANQUETIN at 2.30 p.m. — Accommodation good. — Men billeted in barns. —	2/3
	29th		Cleaning of billets and surrounding area. Arm Drill and Inspection.	2/3
	30th		Squad Drill. Range practices. Gun Drill. Practice in loading and unloading of packsaddlery. 3 O.R's reinforcements.	2/5
	31st		Inspection by B.C. 153rd Infantry Brigade. —	2/5

A Cooper Lieut. for Capt.
COMDG. 153RD COY. M.G. CORPS.

153RD COMPANY, MACHINE GUN CORPS.

153rd Brigade.

51st Division.

153rd MACHINE GUN COMPANY

NOVEMBER 1917.

Attached:-

Account of Operations 20th-24th November'17

Confidential

War Diary
– of –

153rd Company, Machine Gun Corps.

From 1st November to 30th November 1917.

(Volume 40)

WAR DIARY
or
INTELLIGENCE SUMMARY.

(Erase heading not required.)

Volume 40

Army Form C. 2118.

Place	Date	Hour	Summary of Events and Information	Remarks and references to Appendices
WANQUETIN	November 1917			
	1.11.17		Range practices. Attached men mechanism, Gun cleaning and Belt filling	A13.
	2.11.17		Company Drill. Mechanism, Gun Drill. Recreational Games	A13.
	3.11.17		Company Drill and Company Inspections	A13.
	4.11.17		Church Services. —	A13.
	5.11.17		Points B, D and H. firing. Gun cleaning, Visual training Musketry. — Recreational Games. —	A13.
	6.11.17		Gun Drill. — Musketry. — Range Cards. — Gun laying and Recreational Games.	A13.
	7.11.17		2/Lieut E. E. Brown proceeded to Machine Gun Corps Base Depot. Bathing Parade. — M. G. and Rifle practices on short range. —	A13.
	8.11.17		Company training continued	A13.
	9.11.17		Range practices. — Gun cleaning and Belt filling	A13.
	10.11.17		Nos 2 and 4 Sections engaged in Brigade Tactical Exercises. — Nos 1 and 3 Sections, miscellaneous training under Section Officers. —	A13.
	11.11.17		Church Services	A13.
	12.11.17		Long range practices	A13.
	13.11.17		Company training continued	A13.

Army Form C. 2118.

WAR DIARY
or
INTELLIGENCE SUMMARY.

(Erase heading not required.)

Instructions regarding War Diaries and Intelligence Summaries are contained in F. S. Regs., Part II. and the Staff Manual respectively. Title pages will be prepared in manuscript.

Place	Date	Hour	Summary of Events and Information	Remarks and references to Appendices
WANQUENTIN	14/11/17		Short Range practices	A/3
	15/11/17		Nos 1, 2 and 3 Sections engaged in Brigade Tactical exercises. No. 4 Section miscellaneous training	A/3
	16/11/17		All guns and gear packed on limbers ready to move off. Company training continued. Transport moved to COURCELLES-LE-COMTE at 8 p.m.	A/3
BEULENCOURT	17/11/17		Company paraded at 8:30 p.m and marched to BEAUMETZ. Entrained at 12 noon and detrained at BAPAUME at 3 p.m. Marched to BEAULEN-COURT arriving in billets there at 5 p.m. Accommodation good.	A/3
			NISSEN HUTS. Transport joined Company at 11:30 p.m.	
METZ	18/11/17		Company paraded at 4 p.m. and marched to BUS. Entrained on light railway at 8 p.m. and arrived in METZ at 11 p.m. Billets consisted of shelters in the village	A/5
COY H Q TRESCAULT	19/11/17		No. 4 Section left METZ at 5 a.m and took over indirect fire positions from 107th Company on Y day. This Section returned slatterly to HAVRINCOURT WOOD to remain in reserve	A/3
	20/11/17		Guns of this Company co-operated in an attack on the enemy system	

Army Form C. 2118.

WAR DIARY
or
INTELLIGENCE SUMMARY.
(Erase heading not required.)

Place	Date	Hour	Summary of Events and Information	Remarks and references to Appendices
COY. H.Q. TRESCAULT.	20.11.17		REFERENCE MAPS:- BOURLON 1/10,000. BEAUCAMP parts of 57c N.E. & S.E. 1/10,000; MARCOING 57c N.E. 1/10,000 of trenches N.E. of TRESCAULT. (S. IN. of CAMBRAI.) ZERO - 6.20 a.m. The Action of M.G's during the attack was as follows:- For the first and second phases of the Brigade Operations 12 guns of the Company were actually employed in Bourk Belgian Brigade Reserve.- The final advance to the RED DOTTED LINE necessitated the employment of the reserve Section, so that during the whole operation all 16 guns of the Company were in Action. The 12 guns attached accompanied Battalions during the first and second phases were given definite objectives and instructions prior to the attack. They came under the Tactical command of Battalion Commanders with whom they were co-operating.- On the morning of Y day the two Sections detailed for Brigade reserve took over positions in the line there occupied by the 107th M.G. Company.- This Section remained in these positions until shortly before ZERO, when it moved into the reserve positions in the S.E. corner of HAVRINCOURT WOOD.-	

Army Form C. 2118.

WAR DIARY
or
INTELLIGENCE SUMMARY.
(Erase heading not required.)

Instructions regarding War Diaries and Intelligence Summaries are contained in F. S. Regs., Part II. and the Staff Manual respectively. Title pages will be prepared in manuscript.

Place	Date	Hour	Summary of Events and Information	Remarks and references to Appendices
COY HQ TRESCAULT	Nov 20/11/17		For the first and second phases guns were plotted as under :—	

1ST PHASE

One Sub Section with 5th Gordon Highlanders on the left and one sub section with the 6th Black Watch on the right.—

2ND PHASE

One Section with 7th Black Watch on the left and one Section with 7th Gordon Highlanders on the right.—

1ST PHASE

The object of the Sub-Section with the 5th Gordon Highlanders was to take up positions on the HINDENBURG FRONT LINE about K.35. A.2.3 so as to defend the left flank with particular reference to ground about 'T' WOOD.— This they did.— The two guns with the 6th Black Watch were instructed to take up positions in the HINDENBURG FRONT LINE about K.35.B.4.5. and strengthen the defence of that line.— 2/LIEUT SIMPSON found on reaching this front that the ground was quite unsuitable. After reconnoitring he decided to mount the two guns in

2353 Wt W.2511/1454 700,000 5/15 D.D.&L. A.D.S.S./Forms/C 2118.

WAR DIARY
or
INTELLIGENCE SUMMARY.

(Erase heading not required.)

Army Form C. 2118.

Place	Date	Hour	Summary of Events and Information	Remarks and references to Appendices
COY HQ TRESCAULT	NOV 1917	20	MOLE TRENCH about Q 29d 5.2 from which position an excellent field of fire could be obtained. These positions were consolidated. **2ND PHASE:** The Section with the 7th Black Watch advanced in rear of that Battalion with instructions to wait about the RAILWAY CUTTING until the HINDENBURG SUPPORT LINE and FLESQUIERES had been taken and to push forward ultimately to HIGH GROUND N of FLESQUIERES for the defence of that village. Unfortunately the Section lost its Officer at the assembly point about ZERO. SGT BRODIE advanced command. This Section advanced and reached the CUTTING with a loss of 3 killed and 4 wounded. The HINDENBURG SUPPORT LINE having been taken, this Section now i/c of 2/LT MOSS advanced to positions in the trench between the CEMETERY and the Left Brigade boundary. The positions were consolidated. Soon after, it became known that the village was not yet in our hands, and three four guns were moved back to positions in the RAILWAY and HIGHLAND CUTTING. Guns remained in these positions during the night 2/A -	QB

Army Form C. 2118.

WAR DIARY
or
INTELLIGENCE SUMMARY.
(Erase heading not required.)

Place	Date	Hour	Summary of Events and Information	Remarks and references to Appendices
COY HQ TRESCAULT	NOV 1917 21.		The guns with the 7th Gordon Highlanders were instructed to reach the HINDENBURG SUPPORT LINE when the village was in our hands in the same way as the Section with the Battalion on the left. On arrival at the RAILWAY the Officer i/c LIEUT MD MACNAUGHTON M.C. went forward to reconnoitre, leaving his Sergt. with instructions to follow later. LIEUT MACNAUGHTON found FLESQUIERES still in the enemy's hands and became involved in a bombing attack along the trench leading to FLESQUIERES. Here he led a Section of the 7th Gordons which succeeded in inflicting casualties to the enemy in addition to taking prisoners. This Officer was wounded here. His Section Sergt advanced and all 4 guns were mounted in HINDENBURG SUPPORT. Fighting being still in progress about FLESQUIERES WOOD these guns were able to bring direct fire on the enemy in the wood. Two German guns were also mounted and used here. SGT. DUNSIRE did splendid offensive work. When our troops pushed on to HINDENBURG SUPPORT the two guns in MOLE TRENCH about CHAPEL WOOD it having been reported that the enemy was ^advanced to positions in CHAPEL TRENCH	A15

WAR DIARY
or
INTELLIGENCE SUMMARY.

Army Form C. 2118.

Place	Date	Hour	Summary of Events and Information	Remarks and references to Appendices
Coy. H.Q. TRESCAULT	NOV 1917 21		Still going trouble S of HAVRINCOURT. — On the morning of Nov 21st our troops advanced on FLESQUIERES, which was found to have been evacuated during the night. our convoloaded at line N of the village. The guns with the 7th B.H. were advanced to positions N of the village about K.17.d.9.6. Two of the guns with the 7th G.H. advanced to positions at L.13.c.4.5.— The remaining two with the Bourne guns were left in HINDEN- BURG SUPPORT LINE. — The 5th G.H. and the 6th R.H. having now advanced to the DOTTED RED LINE, the reserve section which during the previous afternoon had been brought to TRESCAULT and then in position in CHAPEL TRENCH and MOLE TRENCH advanced in rear of these Battalions. — On the left two guns were placed in position on the stud about K.6.d.3.7 and two about K.12.a.4.8. — A little later in the day one of the former guns was moved back to the rear position and	GB

WAR DIARY
or
INTELLIGENCE SUMMARY.

(Erase heading not required.)

Army Form C. 2118.

Place	Date	Hour	Summary of Events and Information	Remarks and references to Appendices
COY HQ IN THE LINE	November 1917. 21/23		The two Guns were placed in the valley about K.12.d.9.1. After the night the Sections advanced to positions in the vicinity of La' JUSTICE FARM near of the RED DOTTED LINE. The positions were as follows L.1.D.6.3; L.2.C.1.3; L.2.C.3.0 and L.8.A.1.8. Later the gun at L.2.C.3.0 was moved to about L.1.D.3.0. This gun was the first named commanding the whole of the valley as far as ANNEUX. – During the 22nd and 23rd more advantageous positions were reconnoitred, and the final disposition of the guns was as follows:-	

L.2.C.2.3   K.12.a.9.7   L.13.c.5.5   K.17.d.9.6
L.8.A.1.8   K.12.b.1.7   L.13.c.1.4   K.17.b.9.2
L.1.d.6.3   K.12.b.9.2 (2 Guns)   K.18.d.5.6   K.17.d.5.7
L.1.d.3.0   K.18.d.2.4   K.17.b.4.8.-

During the operation of 23rd November orders were received to stand by in readiness to move at about noon.- Pack animals were therefore allotted to Sections with which they

WAR DIARY
or
INTELLIGENCE SUMMARY.
(Erase heading not required.)

Army Form C. 2118.

Place	Date	Hour	Summary of Events and Information	Remarks and references to Appendices
COY H.Q. IN THE LINE	Nov. 1917 23rd		Received from the 23rd orders were received to concentrate all guns on La JUSTICE FARM. This was speedily accomplished.	A5
	24th		The Brigade was withdrawn on the early hours of the 24th and proceeded to TRESCAULT being accommodated in bivouacs. 2/LT M°OSS was wounded during the withdrawal. Detained at ASCHEUX. Marched to YTRES and entrained at 9pm	A13
	25th		and marched to billets in FORCEVILLE arriving at 7am. Clearing of guns + gear. Total casualties during tour in line - 3 Officers and 13 O.R.	
	26th		KILLED 4, DIED OF WOUNDS 1, WOUNDED 7, 17 O.R's joined from BASE DEPOT. Cleaning up finished. 2/Lieut L.V.H. GINGELL and 2/LIEUT G.R. HAMILTON joined from BASE DEPOT.	A13 A13
	27th		Company training commenced. Arm and gun drill etc. — 1 O.R. evac. sick.	A13
	28th		Company training continued.	A13
	29th		Do.	A13
	30th		Marched to ACHEUX and entrained at 6 p.m. Detained at BAPAUME and arrived in billets near LECHELLE at 3.10 a.m = 1.12.17.	A13

A Boyce Capt
Temp Commdg 153rd Coy M.G. Corps.

153rd Company, Machine Gun Corps.

Action of Machine Guns during Operations S.W. of CAMBRAI. 20-11-17 to 24-11-17.

Maps: Baucamp 1:10,000.
Marcoing 57.C NE4 1:10,000.
Bourlon 57.C NE 2 1:10,000.

1. For the first and second phases of the Brigade Operations 12 Machine Guns of 153rd M.G. Company were actually employed, four being held in Brigade Reserve. The final advance to the red dotted Line necessitated the employment of the reserve Section so that during the whole operation all 16 guns of the Company were in action.

2. The 12 guns which accompanied Battalions during the first and second phase were given definate objectives, and instructions prior to the attack. They came under the tactical command of the Battalion Commanders with whom they were co-operating.

3. On the morning of 'Y' day the Section detailed for Brigade Reserve took over positions in the Line occupied by the 107th M.G. Company. The Section remained in these positions until shortly before Zero, when it moved into the reserve position in the S.E. corner of HAVRINCOURT WOOD.

4. For the first and second phases guns were alloted as under:-

   First Phase:
   One sub-section with 5th Gordon Highlanders on the left, and one subsection with 6th Black Watch on the right.

   Second Phase:
   One Section with 7th Black Watch on the left and one Section with 7th Gordon Highlanders on the right.

5. **First Phase.**

   1. The object of the sub-section with the 5th Gordon Highlanders was to take up positions in the HINDENBURG Front line about K 35 a 2 3, so as to defend the left flank with particular reference to ground about 'T' WOOD. This was done.

   2. The two guns with the 6th Black Watch were instructed to take up positions in the HINDENBURG FRONT LINE about K 35 b. 4. 5 and strengthen the defence of the line. Sec/Lieut Simpson found on reaching these positions that the ground was quite unsuitable. He therefore reconnoitred and consulted with Capt. Lindsay, 6th Black Watch. It was decided to mount the two guns in MOLE TRENCH about Q 29. d. 5 2. from which position an

excellent field of fire could be obtained. The positions were consolidated.

6. Second Phase.

1. The Section with the 7th Black Watch advanced in rear of that Battalion with instructions to wait about the RAILWAY CUTTING until the HINDENBURG SUPPORT LINE and FLESQUIERES had been taken and to push forward ultimately to High ground W. of FLESQUIERES for the defence of that village. Unfortunately this Section lost its Officer at the assembly point about ZERO. Sgt Brodie assumed command. The Section advanced and reached the cutting. They lost 3 killed and 4 wounded however. The HINDENBURG SUPPORT LINE having been taken, the Section now in charge of 2/Lieut Moss advanced to positions in that Trench between the CEMETERY and the left Brigade boundary. The positions were consolidated. Soon after, it became known that the village was not yet in our hands, and these four guns were moved back to positions in the RAILWAY and HIGHLAND CUTTING, two positions at each being consolidated. The guns remained in these positions during the night 2/A.

2. The guns with the 7th Gordon Highlanders were instructed to reach the HINDENBURG SUPPORT LINE when the village was in our hands, in the same way as the Section with the Battalion on the left. On arrival at the RAILWAY the Officer in charge LIEUT W.D. MACNAUGHTON M.C. went forward to reconnoitre the found FLESQUIERES still in the enemys hands and became involved in a bombing attack along the Trench leading to FLESQUIERES. He led a Section of the 7th Gordons which succeeded in causing casualties to the enemy in addition to taking prisoners. This Officer was wounded however and was obliged to go down. His Section Sergt, thinking the time opportune for advance did so all four guns being mounted in the HINDENBURG SUPPORT. Fighting being still in progress about FLESQUIERES WOOD, these guns were able to bring direct fire on the enemy in the wood. Two German guns in the trench were also mounted and manned and used against the enemy. Sgt Dunsire here did splendid offensive work. Our troops had pushed on to the HINDENBURG SUPPORT LINE and the two guns left back in MOLE TRENCH, advanced to positions in CHAPEL TR. about CHAPEL WOOD, it having been reported that the enemy was still giving trouble S. of HAVRINCOURT.

7. On the morning of NOVR 21. our troops advanced on FLESQUIERES, which was found to have been evacuated by the enemy during the night and consolidated a line N of the village. The guns with the 7th Black Watch were advanced

to positions at L13C.4.5 and K18.d.8.6. The remaining two with the two German Guns were left in HINDENBURG SUPPORT LINE.

8. The 5th Gordon Highlanders and the 6th Black Watch having now advanced to the DOTTED RED LINE the reserve Section which during the previous afternoon had been brought to TRESCAULT, and the 4 guns in position in CHAPEL TRENCH and MOLE TRENCH advanced in rear of these Battalions.

9. On the left two guns were placed in position on the spur about K6.d.3.7 and two guns about K12.a.7.8. A little later in the day one of the former guns was moved back to the rear position, and the two guns there placed in the VALLEY about K12.B.9.1. for its defence & the defence of batteries.

10. On the right the Section advanced to positions in the vicinity of LA' JUSTICE FARM, in rear of the RED DOTTED LINE. These positions were as follows:- L1D.6.3; L2C.1.3; L2C.3.0; and L8.A.1.8. Later the gun at L2C.3.0 was moved to about L1D.3.0. This gun and the first named commanded the whole of the valley as far as ANNEUX.

11. During the 22nd and 23rd November more advantageous positions were reconnoitred. The final disposition of guns in this defensive line was as follows:- L2C.2.3; L8.a.1.8; L1d.6.3; L1d.3.0; K12.a.9.7; K12.b.1.7; K12.b.9.2 (2) L13.c.5.5 L13.C.1.4; K18.d.5.6; K18.d.2.4; K17.d.9.6; K17.b.9.2; K17.b.5.7; K17.b.4.8.

12. During the afternoon of Nov.r 23rd, orders were received to stand by in readiness to move at short notice. Pack animals were therefore alloted to Sections with which they remained. On the night of the 23rd, orders were received to concentrate all guns on LA' JUSTICE. This was speedily accomplished. The Company remained at this point until the Brigade was withdrawn in the early hours of the 24th.

Pack animals were used for all movements of guns after the first phase. They proved invaluable. Guns were got into position with liberal supplies of ammunition and water and the men arrived at their objectives in splendid fighting condition. Moreover the movement of guns was considerably expedited.

153rd COMPANY,
MACHINE GUN CORPS.
No.
Date. 27-11-17.

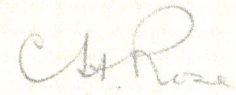

COMDG. 153RD COY. M.G. CORPS.
MAJOR.

Confidential

War Diary

— of —

153rd Company, Machine Gun Corps.

From 1st December 1917 to 31st December 1917.

(Volume 42).

Army Form C. 2118.

Confidential

WAR DIARY
or
INTELLIGENCE SUMMARY.
(Erase heading not required.)

Volume 2.

Instructions regarding War Diaries and Intelligence Summaries are contained in F.S. Regs., Part II. and the Staff Manual respectively. Title pages will be prepared in manuscript.

Place	Date December 1917	Hour	Summary of Events and Information	Remarks and references to Appendices
LECHELLE	1st		Marched to FREMICOURT. Arrived at 7.30 p.m., and were accommodated in Nissen Huts.	
FREMICOURT	2nd	4.45pm	Paraded at 4.45 p.m. and proceeded to the Line. Took over from 163rd M.G. Company. The guns were distributed in the sector as follows:—	
			2 Guns were placed in forward positions at D 24 a 90.55.	
			2 Guns at D 24 c 85.10 (Sunken Road)	
			2 " " D 29 c 15.90 " D 27 a 45.30 (" ")	
			2 " " D 22 c 55.50	
			1 Gun was mounted near J.4.a.5.6 for use against hostile aircraft.	
			Company Headquarters were situated at J.4.a.5.5.	
	3rd		Improvement of positions commenced. No firing done.	
	4th		Enemy shelled in vicinity of positions at D 24 a and RABBIT TRENCH	
COY.HQ. IN THE LINE	5th		During the night of 4th/5th the following moves took place:—	
			The two forward guns were withdrawn at 4.30 a.m. along with 1 gun D 23 d 9.8. (This gun was placed in position during the night of 3rd/4th.) This withdrawal was carried out in conjunction with Infantry retro in accordance with plans withdrew to the OLD BRITISH FRONT LINE. The remaining	

Army Form C. 2118.

WAR DIARY
or
INTELLIGENCE SUMMARY.
(Erase heading not required.)

Instructions regarding War Diaries and Intelligence Summaries are contained in F. S. Regs. Part II. and the Staff Manual respectively. Title pages will be prepared in manuscript.

Place	Date	Hour	Summary of Events and Information	Remarks and references to Appendices
	December 1917			
COY. H.Q. IN THE LINE	5th		Gun teams were relieved by Guns of the 153rd Company. M.G. Coys, on the position stated. Sections, on relief, moved back to FAVREUIL (N. of BAPAUME independently and were accomodated in No. 5 CAMP. The last Section arrived in Camp at 8.30 p.m.	W.D.A.S. W.D.A.S.
FAVREUIL	6th		General clear up of Gun Gear, Equipment, Clothing etc. Company paraded at 3.30 p.m. and proceeded to LOCH CAMP, FREMICOURT, arriving about 5p.m. Accomodation: Huts and Tents. — Front of own Camp was bombed by hostile aircraft. — The following casualties caused:- A/SERGT. WILLIAMS and PTE FERGUSSON killed and 16 ORs wounded.	W.D.A.S. W.D.A.S. W.D.A.S.
FREMICOURT	7th		General clean up. — Company training resumed.	W.D.A.S.
	8th		Company training continued. Huts and Tents sandbagged round bottom as a precaution against bombs.- 1 OR rejoined from Hospital	W.D.A.S.
	9th		Company training continued.	W.D.A.S.
	10th		Company proceeded to line and took over positions from the 152nd M.G. Company.- The position of the guns was as follows:- 3 Guns of No. 1 SECTION in positions at T5d 9.3, T5d 4.5, and J5C 60.05.	W.D.A.S.

2353 Wt. W3544/1454 700,000 5/15 D. D. & L. A.D.S.S. Forms/C. 2118.

Army Form C. 2118.

WAR DIARY
or
INTELLIGENCE SUMMARY.
(Erase heading not required.)

Place	Date	Hour	Summary of Events and Information	Remarks and references to Appendices
COY H.Q. IN THE LINE	December 1917			
	10th		1 Gun of N° 1 SECTION in position at D29c.10.31.	
			3 Guns of N° 2 SECTION IN RESERVE (BEAUMETZ - MORCHIES LINE)	
			1 Gun " " 2 " in FORWARD SUPPORT POSITION	
			4 " " 3 " D27d 3·8 (2guns); D29d on 1, and D22.c.2.3.	
			" " " 4 " J5 b.5.4. and J5 A.1.9	
			2 Guns of " 4 " IN RESERVE LINE	
			1 " " 4 " HERRING SUPPORT (at D29c.4..2)	
			Transport and Stores housed at FREMICOURT.	
			Position unchanged. - 2 of our patrols were brought down and landed in	
	11th		NO MAN'S LAND about D29d.5.5. Informants carried out to engineer-	
			-ments. Un gun from RESERVE was placed in position about K7a.5.5.	
	12th		Artillery activity on both sides were normal. STAND TO was	
			shelled with 5.9s between 2 a.m. and 3.30 a.m. New emplacement complet-	
			-ed at K7a.5.5. - 3000 rounds fired on D10 c.4.4. between 10 p.m. and midnight	
			3 O.R.s wounded	
	13th		3000 rounds fired on D16 b.7.8; D18 d.9.7; and E13.c.3.0 during the night 13/14.	

Army Form C. 2118.

WAR DIARY
or
INTELLIGENCE SUMMARY.
(Erase heading not required.)

Instructions regarding War Diaries and Intelligence Summaries are contained in F. S. Regs., Part II. and the Staff Manual respectively. Title pages will be prepared in manuscript.

Place	Date	Hour	Summary of Events and Information	Remarks and references to Appendices
COY HQ IN THE LINE	December 1917 13th		Artillery showed greater activity during the day. Positions MG Gundy (D.22.c.25.40 and D.22.c.09.40), FISH AV and HERRING SUPPORT were shelled intermittently during the day	f. W.A.S.
	14th		1500 rounds fired on D.6.b.25.90 during the night 13/14th. J.L.S.H. wounded with F.2.H. 89051 Pte N.RONALDS. Killed in Action	f. W.A.S.
	15th		Position remained unchanged. Guns were relieved and positions taken over by 154th MG Company during night of 16/17th. Sections on relief proceed-	f. W.A.S.
	16th		ed to BEUGNY and arrived at 10 a.m. Accommodation NISSEN HUTS. 2 OR	f. W.A.S.
			ranks were wounded during the relief. Total casualties during the tour 1 OR KILLED and 5 ORs WOUNDED.	f. W.A.S.
BEUGNY	17th		General clean up of Guns and Gear	f. W.A.S.
	18th		Gear and cleaning of Equipment and clothing.	f. W.A.S.
	19th		Company training resumed (Squad Drill, Mechanism etc.)	f. W.A.S.
	20th		Company training continued. Firing practice on short range. 19 ORs joined from MG Corps Base Depot. 1 OR evacuated sick.	f. W.A.S.
	21st		Inspection of Company by Commanding Officer. 2 OR returned to Base Depot.	f. W.A.S.

Army Form C. 2118.

WAR DIARY
or
INTELLIGENCE SUMMARY.
(Erase heading not required.)

Instructions regarding War Diaries and Intelligence Summaries are contained in F.S. Regs., Part II. and the Staff Manual respectively. Title pages will be prepared in manuscript.

Place	Date	Hour	Summary of Events and Information	Remarks and references to Appendices
	December 1917			
COY H.Q. BEUGNY	22nd		Preparing of Guns etc, preparatory to going into line. – 8 Guns of the Coy proceeded to the line and took over positions from 154th M.G. Company in the left sub-sector of Doignies Front. The distribution of the guns was as follows:- 3 Guns of N° 4 Section occupied positions in FRONT LINE, (M.G. 5, 6, and 7). 3 " " N° 4 " " " SUPPORT LINE (S4 and S5; R7). 2 " " N° 4 " " " BEAUMETZ – MURCHIE'S LINE were occupied by 1 Team each from N°1 and N°4 Sections. The remaining 8 guns were in Brigade Reserve and were accommodated in BEUGNY. Transport remained at FREMICOURT.	f (a.s.) f (a.s.) f (a.s.) f (a.s.) f (a.s.) f (a.s.)
COY H.Q. IN THE LINE	23rd		Staying out lines of fire, and improving of emplacements. Situation remained quiet. 10 enemy shells fell in J.29.y. between 8pm and 9pm. Position unchanged, and activity on both sides was below normal.	f (a.s.)
	24th		Situation quiet.– No firing done during the period. Improvement of shelters at position at J8 d 25.45.–	f (a.s.)
	25th		Situation quiet and no operations carried out by either side. Visibility unusual.	f (a.s.)

Army Form C. 2118.

Instructions regarding War Diaries and Intelligence Summaries are contained in F. S. Regs., Part II. and the Staff Manual respectively. Title pages will be prepared in manuscript.

WAR DIARY
or
INTELLIGENCE SUMMARY.
(Erase heading not required.)

Place	Date	Hour	Summary of Events and Information	Remarks and references to Appendices
COY. H.Q. IN THE LINE	December 1917			
	25th		and no movement observed.	L.W.S.C.
	26th		1000 rounds were fired on Target D.16.d.10.85 between 12 midnight and 2 a.m. from position T5 (S27d.25.70). Enemy reported to be working trench. Normal activity throughout the day.- 2/Lt N.B. SAVAGE struck off strength.-	L.W.S.C.
	27th		Activity on both sides was below normal, probably on account of the bad visibility. 1000 rounds fired on D.16.d.6.2 between 10 p.m. and 12 midnight.- The following honours and awards appeared on D.R.O. Bar to Military Cross:-	L.W.S.C.
			LIEUT. W.D. MACNAUGHTON M.C.; Military Cross:- T.2/LIEUT. R.W. MOSS D.C.M. Military Medal: Sergt. A. Brodie.- Awards made for gallantry displayed during operations near CAMBRAI on Sept 21/22nd	L.W.S.C.
	28th		1000 rounds fired on D.16.c.4.5 between 12 midnight and 2 a.m. Situation quiet.- Visibility poor.-	L.W.S.C.
	29th		No operations carried out.- Fairly heavy intermittent enemy shelling during the day.- Several light shells fell near positions on D.27.d.3.9.-	L.W.S.C.
	30th		1000 rounds fired on D.16.d.0.2.- A few shells fell near position S.3 (D.28.c.4.5-2.1). Situation unchanged.-	L.W.S.C.

2353 Wt. W2544/1454 700,000 5/15 D. D. & L. A.D.S.S. Forms/C. 2118.

Army Form C. 2118.

WAR DIARY
or
INTELLIGENCE SUMMARY.
(Erase heading not required.)

Instructions regarding War Diaries and Intelligence Summaries are contained in F. S. Regs., Part II. and the Staff Manual respectively. Title pages will be prepared in manuscript.

Place	Date	Hour	Summary of Events and Information	Remarks and references to Appendices
	December 1917.			
COY H Q IN THE LINE	31st		An inter-company relief took place during the evening: No. 1 and 2 Sections relieving No. 2 and 3 Sections who proceeded to Best Billets in BEUGNY. — Relief completed without mishap.	L.W.S.
			Maps References are taken from Sheet 57C N.E. 1 (QUÉANT) 1:10,000.	

J. W. Pinnell, Lieut
Temp. Commdg. 153rd Coy, M.G. Corps.

Confidential

War Diary

— of —

153rd Company, Machine Gun Corps

From 1st January 1918 to 31st January 1918.

Volume 42

Army Form C. 2118.

WAR DIARY
or
INTELLIGENCE SUMMARY.
(Erase heading not required.)

Volume 42

Instructions regarding War Diaries and Intelligence Summaries are contained in F.S. Regs., Part II. and the Staff Manual respectively. Title pages will be prepared in manuscript.

Place	Date	Hour	Summary of Events and Information	Remarks and references to Appendices
	January 1918			
COY H.Q. IN LINE (PRONVILLE SECTOR)	1st		½ Company in BEUGNY relieved ½ Company in Line during night 31/12/17/1/1/18. — Situation unchanged. — Period quiet.	
	2nd		Day Quiet. Reserve Sections in BEUGNY engaged in cleaning of Guns Equipment etc. — 1 O.R. evacuated sick. —	
	3rd		1800 rounds fired on enemy outpost line. — Reserve Sections at Beugny engaged at Mechanism Gun Drill, Squad Drill.	
	4th		2000 rounds fired on fronts on enemy's Lines. Reserve Sections continued with training. Situation unchanged. — Enemy activity below normal.	
	5th		2 Sections in line were relieved by 2 Sections from Reserve in Beugny. Our forward positions were shelled from 9.30p.m to 10 p.m. No damage was done. — No. 36653 L/Cpl Meecham taken on strength. 1 O.R. returned sick.	
	6th		No firing carried out owing to the presence of our working parties and patrols in front. — Reserve Sections continued with training.	
	7th		2000 rounds fired on enemy's Roads and Trenches. — Reserve Sections carried out miscellaneous training. —	
	8th		500 rounds fired on enemy roads. — Situation unchanged and enemy activity nil.	

Army Form C. 2118.

WAR DIARY
or
INTELLIGENCE SUMMARY.
(Erase heading not required.)

Instructions regarding War Diaries and Intelligence Summaries are contained in F. S. Regs., Part II. and the Staff Manual respectively. Title pages will be prepared in manuscript.

Place	Date	Hour	Summary of Events and Information	Remarks and references to Appendices
COY H.Q. IN LINE	January 1918			
	9th		2 Sections in Reserve at BEUGNY relieved 2 Sections on the Line during the night. Company H.Q. shelled. 1000 rounds fired on special targets. 2 O.R's joined from Base Depot – 1 O.R. evac. (Sick.) 1 O.R. wounded.	A.13
	10th		Situation unchanged. 1000 rounds fired on new enemy sap and wire. Reserve Sections engaged in cleaning of Guns, equipment etc. – 1 O.R. evac. Sick.	A.13
	11th		3000 rounds fired on enemy roads and dumps during the night. Day quiet. 4 O.R's reinforcements joined from M.G.C. Base Depot.	A.13
	12th		Normal activity. 2000 rounds fired on Enemy Tracks and Light Railways. Miscellaneous training was carried out by Sections in Reserve. 2 Sections from reserve relieved 2 Sections on the Line during the night.	A.13
	13/14th		2000 rounds fired on new enemy Out-front Line.	A.13
	14th		Situation unchanged. Little activity on either side owing to bad weather. 1,500 rounds fired on enemy sap. Reserve Sections continued with training.	A.13
	15th		1000 rounds fired on Enemy Tracks and Dumps during night.	A.13
	16th		1000 on enemy wire during night of 16/17th.	A.13

Army Form C. 2118.

WAR DIARY
or
INTELLIGENCE SUMMARY.
(Erase heading not required.)

Instructions regarding War Diaries and Intelligence Summaries are contained in F. S. Regs., Part II. and the Staff Manual respectively. Title pages will be prepared in manuscript.

Place	Date	Hour	Summary of Events and Information	Remarks and references to Appendices
	January 1918			
COY H Q IN THE LINE	17th		2 Sections in the line relieved by 2 Sections from reserve in BEUGNY. 1000 rounds fired on enemy wire, where working parties suspected. Activity on both sides was below normal.	C13
	18th		No firing was carried out during period. Sections in Reserve were busy with training.	C13
BEUGNY	19th		Company relieved by 18th Machine Gun Company. Sections in line proceeded to billets in BEUGNY. Reserve Sections moved back to FREMICOURT. 1 O.R. from hosp: 4 OR to Field Amb:	C13, C13
"	20th		Day spent in cleaning up, 154th M.G. Company.	C13
COURCELLES LE COMTE	21st		Company marched from BEUGNY at 12.noon and reached COURCELLES LE COMTE at 4.p.m. Billets-Nisson Huts. Camp in a deep condition. and in bad repair.	C13
"	22nd		Cleaning and improving of camp and repairing of huts etc. 1 O.R. rejoined from Hospital.	C13
"	23rd		Company training commenced. Squad Drill, Inspection of Guns, Lectures etc. Rifle Exercises, Lectures. 3 O.R. from Base Depot.	C13
"	24th		Company training continued. 1 O.R. returned to 41st Infty Brigade HQrs.	C13

A5834 Wt. W4973/M687 750,000 8/16 D. D. & L. Ltd. Forms/C.2118/13

Army Form C. 2118.

WAR DIARY
or
INTELLIGENCE SUMMARY.
(Erase heading not required.)

Instructions regarding War Diaries and Intelligence Summaries are contained in F.S. Regs., Part II. and the Staff Manual respectively. Title pages will be prepared in manuscript.

Place	Date	Hour	Summary of Events and Information	Remarks and references to Appendices
	January 1918			
COURCELLES LE COMTE	25th		Range practices on short range. Lectures. 10R (casualty) rejoined. 1R evac. Sick	A/3
	26th		Testing (chiefly) Gas Respirators. Medals Sgt Taylor & Corpl Docto off. (Special Course at Duntulm)	A/3
	27th		Commanding Officers inspection of Company. Church Parades. Hostels Aircraft passing over actively several times during night. 10R evac Sick	A/3
	28th		Gun Drill, Chronometer, Planning and traversing dial T.A. and spares tests. Lectures.	A/3
	29th		Range practices with rifles. Hostile Aircraft again active in neighbourhood.	A/3
	30th		Tactical Exercises - Use of ground and cover etc.	A/3
	31st		Long practices on short ranges.	A/3
	1.2.18.			

A Pyre Lieut for Captain
Commanding 153rd Coy. M.G. Corps.

W 25

Confidential

War Diary

— of —

153rd Company, Machine Gun Corps.

From 1st February 1918 to 28th February 1918

(Volume 43.)

Army Form C. 2118.

WAR DIARY
or
INTELLIGENCE SUMMARY. Volume

(Erase heading not required.)

Instructions regarding War Diaries and Intelligence Summaries are contained in F.S. Regs., Part II. and the Staff Manual respectively. Title pages will be prepared in manuscript.

Place	Date	Hour	Summary of Events and Information	Remarks and references to Appendices
COURCELLES-LE-COMTE	February 1918			
	1st		Company engaged at Long Range Practice.	C+R
	2nd		Company paraded to bid farewell to 15th Gordon Highlanders Practice Brigade	
			Ceremonial Parade during forenoon	C+R
	3rd		Church Parades	C+R
	4th	8.30	Company paraded and took part in Defence Scheme (Defence of village of Courcelles)	
			a) during forenoon. Recreational Games. 1 OR rejoined from 47th RTC (Reg)	C+R
	5th	10	Company training continued. Lectures and Recreational Games. 1 OR to Hosp!	
			U.K. (furlough on leave)	C+R
	6th		Company engaged in a Tactical Exercise during forenoon (Defence of village of COURCELLES-LE-COMTE). 1 OR evacuated sick.	C+R
	7th		Company training continued. LIEUT BRYCE and 2/LIEUT HAMILTON to Hospital	C+R
	8th		Company training continued. Inspection of Company by Brigadier General A.T. BECKWITH Commanding 153rd Infantry Brigade at 10.30 a.m and by Major General G. MONTAGUE HARPER, Commanding, 51st (H) Division at 11 a.m	C+R
			Marching etc prior to moving.	C+R

Army Form C. 2118.

WAR DIARY
or
INTELLIGENCE SUMMARY.
(Erase heading not required.)

Instructions regarding War Diaries and Intelligence Summaries are contained in F. S. Regs., Part II. and the Staff Manual respectively. Title pages will be prepared in manuscript.

Place	Date	Hour	Summary of Events and Information	Remarks and references to Appendices
	February 1918			
COURCELLES -LE-COMTE	9th	7.30am	Marched to ACHIET-LE-GRAND. Entrained and moved by Light Railway to BEUGNY. Hence by road to SHAKLETON CAMP, LEBUCQUIERE. Transport moved by road. Accommodation - Nissen Huts. Nos 1, 3 and 4 Sections proceeded to lend and relieved guns of 18th M.G. Company in PROUVILLE SECTOR during the night.	
	9/10th		Disposition of Guns as follows :- 4 Guns of No. 1 Section in SUPPORT LINE. 4 Guns of 4 Section in INTERMEDIATE LINE. 2 to Guns of No. 3 Section remained at Company H.Q. ready to mount in BEAUMETZ-MORCHIES LINE at half an hours notice. Company H.Q. situated in SUNKEN ROAD near MORCHIES (1/2 a 8.7). Relief completed at 10.4pm.	CWR
COY. H.Q.	10		Situation unchanged. Activity on both sides normal. No firing occurred and 12 M.G. Emplacements in ROBIN SUPPORT (D29.c.20.80) commenced. Journey-	CWR
IN THE LINE			ment. No. 2 Section and details moved to BEUGNY and took over accommodation vacated by 18th M.G. Company. 2/LIEUT W.B. SAVAGE rejoined from M.G.B. Base Depot.	CWR
	11th		Moved quiet. No firing down.	CWR

Army Form C. 2118.

WAR DIARY
or
INTELLIGENCE SUMMARY.
(Erase heading not required.)

Instructions regarding War Diaries and Intelligence Summaries are contained in F. S. Regs., Part II. and the Staff Manual respectively. Title pages will be prepared in manuscript.

Place	Date	Hour	Summary of Events and Information	Remarks and references to Appendices
	February 1918			
COY H.Q.			Enemy Artillery showed greater activity than usual. About 20 rounds H.E. shells	
MORCHIES	12th		fell near M.G. position. M.G. fired at 9 a.m. No damage was done. C.M.R	
			Fired 3000 rounds on Enemy Trenches etc in D.16.d., D.23.a. and D.30.a.	C.M.R
	13th		during night of 12/13th. Day quiet.	C.M.R
	14th		Exceptionally quiet during period. Our M.G. fired 1500 rounds on D.16.C.57.20	C.M.R
			during night 13/14th.	C.M.R
	15th		Situation unchanged. Fired 3000 rounds on Enemy Tracks in D.16.C; D.17.c	C.M.R
			and D.23.a. Period quiet.	
	16th		Inter Section reliefs already were carried out on the night 15/16th :-	
			No. 2 Section relieved No. 1 Section in the SUPPORT LINE.	
			No. 3 Section relieved No. 4 Section in the INTERMEDIATE LINE.	
			No. 4 Section moved to C.H.Q. and No. 1 Section to BEUGNY	C.M.R
	17th		Weather favourable and slightly increased Artillery activity through active.	
			2 Enemy machines shot down in this Sector today. 4,500 rounds fired on	
			Targets in D.16.a and d; D.23.a. and D.24.a.	C.M.R

Army Form C. 2118.

WAR DIARY
or
INTELLIGENCE SUMMARY.
(Erase heading not required.)

Instructions regarding War Diaries and Intelligence Summaries are contained in F. S. Regs., Part II. and the Staff Manual respectively. Title pages will be prepared in manuscript.

Place	Date	Hour	Summary of Events and Information	Remarks and references to Appendices
	February 1918			
COMPANY H.Q.	18th		Much aerial activity on both sides. Fired 3000 rounds on Targets in D15d and D17c during night 17/18th. — 1 O.R. evacuated to 200.L	C.+R
MORCHIES	19th		Fired 1,250 rounds on Enemy Tracks in D15d and D17c during night 19/20th. 1 Sergt Goldard joined from M.S.G Base Depot.	C.+R
	20th		Weather unfavourable and situation quiet. — No. 4 Section mounted 2 guns in BEAUMETZ—MORCHIES LINE at T14 & T7.L — 300 rounds were fired by new M.Gs on Targets D16d, D17d, and D23 art. (Enemy Trenches etc.)	C.+R
	21st		Sec intra - Section relief was completed as follows :-	
			No. 4 Section relieved No. 2 Section in SUPPORT LINE	
			No. 1 " " " 3 " " INTERMEDIATE LINE	
			No. 2 Section took over 2 positions in B.M. LINE at T14 & T7.L. and 2 Guns remained at C.H.Q. — No 3 Section returned to BEUGNY.	C.+R
	22nd		Period normal. Weather favourable and usual aerial activity. Fired 2000 rounds on Q.23.L during night 21st/22nd	C.+R
	23rd		Slightly increased artillery activity. Weather good. Fired 3000 rounds on Targets in D.15.d and D17c during night 23/24th. 3 O.R. reinforcements joined	C.+R

Army Form C. 2118.

WAR DIARY
or
INTELLIGENCE SUMMARY.
(Erase heading not required.)

Instructions regarding War Diaries and Intelligence Summaries are contained in F.S. Regs. Part II. and the Staff Manual respectively. Title pages will be prepared in manuscript.

Place	Date	Hour	Summary of Events and Information	Remarks and references to Appendices
	February 1918			
COMPANY	23rd		Front M.G. Head Depot. 1 OR wounded. 3 OR's evacuated sick.	C.M.R
H.Q. MORCHIES	24th		Situation unchanged. Our M.Gs fired 3000 rounds on targets in D.15.d and D.17.c during night 23/24th. 4 OR evacuated sick.	C.M.R
	25th		Day quiet. 1500 rounds fired on targets moving in D.17.c. 2 Observation Posts unchanged. 3000	C.M.R
	26th		Artillery of both sides slightly more active. Situation unchanged. 3000 rounds fired on targets in D.16.d and D.17.c (Enemy Tracks) during night 25/26th.	C.M.R
	27th		Day quiet. 1500 rounds fired on targets in D.21.b during night 25/26th.	C.M.R
	28th		Situation unchanged. Fired 3000 rounds on targets in D.17.c and d during night 27/28.	C.M.R
			Maps referenced are taken from QUEANT 1:10,000; HERMIES 1:10,000 and MOEUVRES SPECIAL SHEET 1:20,000	

Captain
Commanding 153rd Coy. M.G. Corps.

www.ingramcontent.com/pod-product-compliance
Lightning Source LLC
Chambersburg PA
CBHW081429160426

43193CB00013B/2230